Poems From Tyne & Wear

Edited by Annabel Cook

 Young**Writers**

First published in Great Britain in 2008 by:
Young Writers
Remus House
Coltsfoot Drive
Peterborough
PE2 9JX
Telephone: 01733 890066
Website: www.youngwriters.co.uk

SB ISBN 978-1 84431 468 3

Foreword

Young Writers was established in 1991 and has been passionately devoted to the promotion of reading and writing in children and young adults ever since. The quest continues today. Young Writers remains as committed to the nurturing of poetic and literary talent as ever.

This year's Young Writers competition has proven as vibrant and dynamic as ever and we are delighted to present a showcase of the best poetry from across the UK and in some cases overseas. Each poem has been selected from a wealth of *Little Laureates* entries before ultimately being published in this, our sixteenth primary school poetry series.

Once again, we have been supremely impressed by the overall quality of the entries we have received. The imagination, energy and creativity which has gone into each young writer's entry made choosing the poems a challenging and often difficult but ultimately hugely rewarding task - the general high standard of the work submitted ensured this opportunity to bring their poetry to a larger appreciative audience.

We sincerely hope you are pleased with this final collection and that you will enjoy *Little Laureates Poems From Tyne & Wear* for many years to come.

Contents

Barnes Junior School

Kate Hindmarch (10)	1
Thomas Ward (10)	1
Daisy Bell (10)	2
Dominic Copeland (10)	2
Louise Brown (10)	3
Rebecca Steinberg (10)	3
Reece Seafield-Smith (10)	4
James Myers (10)	4
Kelsey Fowler (10)	5
Emily Pretty (11)	5
Georgia-Rose Spargo (10)	6
Hannah Adams (11)	6
Christopher Wright (11)	7
Fiona Sopp (10)	7
Holly Kilner (11)	8
Harry Price (10)	8
Lucy-Rhiannon Forster (10)	9
Hannah Tullock (11)	9
Andrew Brewster (10)	10
Georgia Smith (9)	10
Charlotte Baron 11)	11
Emily Lonsdale (11)	11
Elliott Young (10)	12
Jade Hughes (10)	12
Rebecca Dewhurst (10)	13
Lidya Balaban (8)	13
Ellie Campbell (10)	14
Adam Johnson (10)	14
Lucy Ellis (10)	15
Hannah Todd (10)	15
Victoria Hunter (10)	16
Cameron Wright (10)	16
Tiffany Eadie (8)	16
Amy Thompson (10)	17
Sally Martin (10)	17
Callum Houghton (10)	18
Daniel Waugh (10)	18
Sana Baber (10)	19

Hannah Stanger (10)   19
Lauren Coates (11)   20
Brittany Wood (10)   20
Andrew Burns (10)   21
Kuzi Bwanya (10)   21
Sacha Hawes (9)   22
Charlotte Dunn (11)   22
Samuel James Eley (10)   23
Sofenna Lowe (11)   23
Matthew Trimble (8)   24
Hollie Rosborough (10)   24

Bede Burn Primary School
Ashleigh Williamson & Rachael Dawson (11)   24
Chloe Parvin & Alice Carr (10)   25
Amy Farrell & Adam Curry (10)   25
Sarah Mullin & Gabrielle Davidson (10)   26
Sarah Jane Bambrough (9)   26
Ross Dunn (8)   26
Aiden Coyne (8)   27
Katie Quinn (8)   27
Madeleine Brown (9)   28
Harley McCourt (8)   28
Ilicia Mason & Zoe Turnbull (10)   28
Jackson Parker (8)   29
Amber Lea (8)   29
Alice Atkinson & Jessica Birch (10)   30
Emma Gardner (9)   30
Christian Johnson-Richards & Ben Stevenson (10)   30
Ben Hall & Sophie Downie (10)   31
Bethany Watkinson & Sam Drewery (10)   31
Adam Johnston & Jack Syrett (10)   31

Cragside Primary School
Jonny Maddick (10)   32
Tamzin Anderson (11)   32
Alexander Martin (10)   33
Lauren Short (10)   33
Aisha Khan (10)   34
Laura Phillips (10)   34
Ryan Holmes (10)   35

Nicole Kortenbach (10)   35
Amy Topping (10)   36

Greenfields Community Primary School
Ben Sutton (9)   36
Dionne Robson (9)   37
James Crooks (10)   37
Ellie Glover (9)   38
Daniel Ferguson (9)   38
Hannah Black (9)   39
Abigail Cook (9)   39
Megan Raffle (9)   40
Matthew O'Donnell (9)   40
Charlotte Anderson (9)   41
Andrew Armstrong (9)   41

John F Kennedy Primary School
Liam Butler (11)   42
Jasmine Charlton (10)   42
Aryan Sheikhalian (10)   43
Chloe Ross (10)   43
Matthew Softley (10)   44
Jordan Taylor (10)   44
Abbie Dixon (10)   45
Alex Boylen (10)   45
Hannah McKinlay (10)   46
Daniel Craigs (10)   46
Emma Noble (10)   47
Emma Dover (10)   47
Emily Marriner (10)   48
Holly Rawson (10)   48
Thea McMullan-Jones (10)   49
Matthew Wylie (11)   49
Jamie Natton (10)   50
Oliver Manley (10)   50
Aaron Monaghan (10)   51
Jamie Drysdale (10)   51
Alexander Cotterill (10)   52
John Petersen (11)   52
Sally Charlton (10)   53
Curtis Borthwick (10)   53

Adam Miskell (10)   54
Sophie Maughan (10)   54
Corey Butters (10)   54
Emma Wylie (11)   55
Sarah Smith (10)   55
Georgia Robison (10)   56

Kingston Park Primary School
Joe Wilson (11)   56
Bethanie Culyer (11)   57
Hannah Pyle (11)   57
Emily Brown (10)   58
Lois Mason (10)   58
Beth Lant (10)   59
Honor Corfield (10)   59
Brandon Cooper (10)   60
Reece Havelock-Brown (10)   60
Amy Dalrymple (11)   61
Jack Robson (10)   61
Rebecca Henry (11)   62
Reema Albalushi (10)   62

Marley Hill Community Primary School
Hannah Hailes (10)   63
Kelsey Madden (10)   64
Mathew Wilson (10)   65
Elissa Mennell (11)   66
Bethany Lowes (10)   67

New Penshaw Primary School
Brian Quinn (11)   67
Chloe Bellas (11)   68
Ryan Hamilton (10)   68
Sharn Hannan (11)   69
Nathan Wilson (10) & Callum Genther (10)   69
Natasha Raymond (10)   69
Nathan Hutchinson (11)   70
Regan Naisbett (10)   70
Kieron Hughes (10)   71
Billy Davison (11)   71
Kenya Allen (11)   71

Dominic Turnbull (11)	72
Kim Mason (11)	72
Abby Johnson (10)	73
Chloe Poulter (10)	73
Eddy Burney (10)	73
Caitlin Vest (10)	74
Jack Ramsden (11)	74
Nathan McMenam (11)	74
Roseann Galloway (11)	75
Michael Layford (11)	75

New York Primary School

Morgan Whitaker (7)	76
Shaunna Jolly (9)	77
Tom Simmonds (8)	78

Redesdale Primary School

Josh Greener (10)	78
Lewis Keogh (11)	79
James Shek (10)	79
Lauren Nicole Goodfellow (10)	79
Alex Forman (11)	80
Amy Sutherland (10)	80
Dominic Ho (11)	81
Ben Durham (9)	81
William Robson (10)	82
Callum-Leslie Weites (10)	82
David Scott (9)	82
Darius Liu (9)	83
Hannah Watson (10)	83
Callum Heppell (10)	83
Emily-Rose Snowdon (10)	84
Sophie Dugdale (10)	84
Melissa Stephenson (10)	84
Jonathan Watson (10)	85
Errin Storey (9)	85
Bethany Relph (11)	85
Becky Weightman-Brierley (9)	86
Andy Chan (10)	86
Natalie Wandless (10)	87
Samantha Wright (9)	87

Jayson Hunt (9)	88
Hannah Carr (10)	88
Michael O'Brien (9)	89
Jamie Hunt (9)	89
John Wright (9)	90
April Horner (10)	90
Joshua McGregor (9)	91
Ryan Orchard (10)	91
Jordan Mishner (9)	92
Alex Lovell (9)	92

St Agnes' School, Crawcrook

Matilda Noble (10)	93
Diane Curry (10)	93
Beth Rutherford (10)	94
Peter Dixon (11)	94
Elisabeth Baker (10)	95
Sophie Howorth (10)	95
Rian McLaughlin (10)	96
Ryan Havery (9)	96
Katherine Milton (9)	97
Ruth Brickland (9)	97
Michaela Bousfield (9)	98
Emily Gray (9)	98
Kathleen Phillips-Buck (9)	99
Joseph Allan (8)	99
Dominic Harrison (9)	100
Kasia Mackay (9)	100
Erin Stutt (9)	101
Philip Butler (9)	101
Alex Wildman (9)	102
Erin Golightly (9)	102
Becky Robinson (9)	103
Christy Bright (9)	103
Jennifer Reynolds (7)	104
Keelan Kellegher (9)	104
Sarah Baker (7)	105
Lucy Roddam (8)	106
Daniel Allan (9)	106
Bethany McLaughlin (7)	107
Harvey Jack (7)	108

Joe Urwin (10)   108
Chantelle Christensen (7)   109
Marlie Corble-Robson (9)   109
Matthe Hamill (7)   110
Katie Stuart-Brown (9)   110
Sophie Thorpe (9)   111
Tom Ellis (9)   111
Lucy King (9)   112
Jackson Maddison (9)   112
William Watson (7)   113
Jack Thompson (9)   113
Lucy May Wood (7)   114
Kayleigh Grant (9)   114
Alice Brown (7)   115
Harry Carver (9)   115
Katie Lawson (7)   116
Bethany Caffrey (10)   116
Corinna Grant (7)   117
Michelle Reid (8)   118
Adam Charlton (10)   118
Faye Parker (7)   119
Sarah Rutherford (7)   120
Izzy Sherborne (10)   120
Georgie Mackay (8)   121
Fabrizio Stifanelli (10)   121
Adam Davidson (7)   122
Bethan Hobson (7)   123
Jenny Hetherington (8)   124
David Guy (8)   124
Megan Dawson (8)   125
Myles Croxford (9)   125
Zhandos Kearney (8)   126
Sean Henry (8)   126
Aimee Stamp (8)   127
Kirsty Wright (8)   127
Megan Rubbi (8)   128
Catherine Baker (8)   128
Michael Harrison (10)   129
Caitlin Gray (10)   129
Brendan Richardson (10)   130
Rachel Findley (10)   130
Jessica Dawson (10)   130

Coleen Mary Huntley (10)   131
Bethany Oliver (10)   131
Charlotte Mann (10)   132
Ricky Macis (10)   132
Elle Croxford (10)   133
Niamph Gilmore (10)   133
Erin Mann (10)   134
Tori Houckham (10)   134

St Catherine's RC Primary School, Sandyford
Stella Robinson (10)   135
Alicia Youens (10)   136
Rebecca Wood (10)   137
Esme Cawley (8)   137
Jasmine Little (9)   138
Lily Rose Oliver (8)   139

St John Bosco Primary School, Sunderland
Josie-Leigh Donkin (9)   140
Dana Deary (9)   140
Caitlin Henderson (9)   141
James Watt (9)   141
Ben Clark (10)   142
Ryan Donnellan (9)   142
Tom Walker (9)   143
Sarah O'Connor (9)   143
Lauren Garner (9)   144

St John Vianney Catholic Primary School, West Denton
Jack Bell (9)   144
Anya Nelson (9)   145
Robyn McNulty (9)   145
Jasmine Kidd (9)   146
Olivia Killen (9)   146
Jack Harrington (10)   146
Adam Barnett (9)   147
Emily Patterson (10)   147
Andrew Coffell (10)   147
Amy Hawkins (10)   148
Emily Davis (9)   148
Emily Armstrong (9)   149

Luke Walton (9)   149
Aimee Duncan (9)   150
Sarah Balmain (9)   150
Jessica Burgess (9)   150
Joanna Hodgson (10)   151
Bree Dalton (9)   151
Emily Walton (9)   151
Jessica Hall (9)   152

St Mary's RC Primary School, Forest Hall
Kate McHugh 10)   152
Zachary Hui (10)   153
Lauren Napier (10)   153

St Mary's RC Primary School, Sunderland
Eleanor Osada (10)   154
Francesca Shanks (10)   155
Daniel Forrest (11)   155
Callum Bradfield (10)   156
Meriel Smithson (10)   157
Daniel Simpson (10)   158
Sam Hope (10)   158

Sea View Primary School
Holly Hazell (9)   159
Dylan Ford (9)   159
Scott Davison (9)   160
Chloe Kingsland (9)   160
Megan Galloway (9)   160
Alisha Kirtley (9)   161
Chloe Stephenson (9)   161
Danielle James (9)   161
Marley Luther (9)   162
Shannon Robinson (9)   162
Stevie Brooks (9)   163
Brandon Riley (9)   163

Valley Road Community Primary School
Joshua Smith (8)   164
Clayton Gough (8)   164

Ryan Ganley (9)   164
Tialeoni Thompson (8)   165
Jimmy Hall (8)   165
Sara Robson (8)   165
Nathan Reay (9)   166
Elle Young (8)   166

The Poems

Neglected Castle

Abandoned and lonely,
The castle stood as still as a statue,
With no one there to keep him company.
Suddenly!

Garden gnomes began to dance and sing,
Music played so gently
And the grass started to wave.
Eyes started blinking,
Witches laughed,
'Haha, haha!'
'It's scary!'
'It's spooky!'

The tongue stuck out
And the arms got closer together,
Then the big, huge mouth watered.
The frantic gates swung open
And then . . .
In came all of the people of the world!

Kate Hindmarch (10)
Barnes Junior School

Farmyard

The morning dew on the farm
Gives way to the morning sun.
All you can hear is the cows
Milking in the byre
And the sheep grazing
On the pasture,
Along with the shire horses
In the field.

Thomas Ward (10)
Barnes Junior School

Springtime

Spring is creeping round the corner
As the sun begins to put on his suncream.
The little lambs are in the field
Playing tag with their friends.

Spring is singing a little song
As the children come out to play.
The spring flowers are in the garden,
Starting to bloom.

Children are coming out to play
In the fields and in the hay.
Summer is starting to come,
People are getting a nice tan.

Baby rabbits are hopping all about,
Chicks are sweeping up their new corn,
Spring is making baby animals,
There is just one more thing to do
And that is turn into spring again.

Daisy Bell (10)
Barnes Junior School

The Killer Storm

The storm had been getting wilder and wilder over days.
It got so torrential, it obliterated the whole town
Like a giant stomping on a sandcastle.
Houses were evacuated and families cried
As the water level rose and flooded the town.
Many people died.
Thunder rocked the town, lightning burned the birds in the sky.
The birds fell to the floor like stones.
The storm could come to your town!

Dominic Copeland (10)
Barnes Junior School

Summer Sun

The summer sun shines down.
The sun loves everyone.
The sun's bright orange nose sparkles.
The sun shines in the clear blue sky.

On the first day of summer,
I get up very early, ready for the sun.
The sun sparkles brightly every day.
The sun doesn't like people that
Just sit in the house all day.

The sun overtakes all of the clouds.
The sun's eyes glisten.
The sun loves it when there are
No clouds in the sky.

The sun loves it when it rains at the same time,
It forms a colourful rainbow.
The sun loves being the sun.

Louise Brown (10)
Barnes Junior School

Rain

Drip, drop, drip, drop, raindrops start to
Jump out of the grey clouds above,
Bouncing onto the ground,
Gradually getting heavier and heavier.

Puddles are lying still on the ground,
Acting like they're dead, but they're not . . . *splash!*
They attack when somebody, or something,
Stands in the trap!

It's time for the rain to go,
The grey clouds turn to white.
Drip . . . drop . . .

Rebecca Steinberg (10)
Barnes Junior School

Seasons

Conkers are kicking themselves off the trees
Waiting for their home to be opened.
The rain stomps down from the grey sky,
Now it turns to winter as the snow
Floods most of the streets.
Suddenly the sun kills the snow.

It becomes spring as the flowers
Jump up from the soil.
The rabbits hop out of their fluffy homes,
The clouds, as they are just born.

As spring ends, summer returns.
As the children enjoy their holidays,
Sunbathing and swimming at the beach.
The flowers obey the sun as it shines brightly,
And children have a relaxing break from teachers.

Reece Seafield-Smith (10)
Barnes Junior School

A Crazy House

While I stand still as a statue
Through the freezing and boiling weather,
I open my great big beady eyes
And watch everything that happens,
And with my tongue
I gobble all the dirt off people's disgusting shoes,
And if my miserable owners don't treat me nicely,
Then I will pull out my hair
And I'll try to drop it on your head.
It will leave a big bump.

So you had better treat your house nicely or . . .
The same could happen to you.

James Myers (10)
Barnes Junior School

A Tree In A Storm

I'm like a guard standing tall,
Swaying from side to side,
Dancing to thunder's song,
Grabbing humans' objects that fly around.

I feel like blitzing away
To see my wooden family,
Who sit like scarecrows
Day after day.

My arms stick out like a pointy dagger,
I'm determined to poke you with my fingers.
As my hair blows dramatically,
I start to do stretches as I wobble around.

After the storm
I woke up on the floor
To find I was snapped in two,
Dying . . . away . . . slowly . . .

Kelsey Fowler (10)
Barnes Junior School

Summer Sun

The summer sun is glistening in the sky,
The summer sun is high in the sky
The summer sun is fading away,
Everyone is going home again.

The summer sun comes again,
Everyone is playing in the sun
The sun shines high in the sky,
Everyone loves the sun.

The summer sun shines and shines,
Everyone piling on the suncream
Kids playing in the sea.

Emily Pretty (11)
Barnes Junior School

Stars

Prancing on the moon,
Shining in the night,
Little stars begin to fly,
Watching the world go by,
Hurtling on to Mars like athletes,
Playing through the night,
Little stars flying gracefully across space
Like swans on a lake,
Glistening like diamonds,
Dancing everywhere
Without a single care,
The moon shining on their skin,
Like the sun blazing on a pond,
After meeting the aliens on Planet Mars.

Georgia-Rose Spargo (10)
Barnes Junior School

The Moon

High above the world I am,
Round the Earth I spin.
I'm a satellite, but not an artificial one!
Small but proud I stand,
Spinning while time flies by.
The stars continuously wink at me as I fly by.
Man treads on my light and dark side,
And creates extra craters in me,
But I don't like it.
Into the darkness I fade,
But I will be back tonight,
And fly round the world once again.

Hannah Adams (11)
Barnes Junior School

The Bin

I sit in the damp corner,
Never fully clear.
When the humans put me outside,
Wasps annoyingly buzz around me . . .
The lonely bin.

I am forced to look one way
And eat rubbish,
And possibly the odd cornflake or two.
I see dogs sniff at me . . .
The lonely bin.

I can even eat dead plants,
But they're not lively.
I even wear a brown coat to eat them.
I think of my family
Who got separated from me
At the store.

Christopher Wright (11)
Barnes Junior School

Winter

Taking over autumn,
I frost bitterly through the air.
I breathe awfully cold icicles
Onto the crooked trees.
I spit pure white snow,
Filling in footprints,
And cause unhappiness.
But then,
My water supply freezes
And suddenly,
My icy fun is over.

Fiona Sopp (10)
Barnes Junior School

The Life Of A Toy Soldier

Marching and saluting, high up in the bedroom,
He stands there silently and sleeping,
Waiting for the night.
As it comes, he awakens,
Ready for the hard work he faces,
Shouting to his citizens, he barks his orders.

As the battle of a lifetime looms ahead,
He polishes his rusty skills,
But once the day comes round again,
Slowly he makes the treacherous
Climb to his shelf.

Always like a guard dog, defending his surroundings,
Until that day, oh that horrible day,
When he died in vain
In the struggle for freedom.

Now the bedroom is silent,
Nothing comes alive.
His army is dead,
So the struggle is no more.

Holly Kilner (11)
Barnes Junior School

The Sun

His fiery eye follows my every move,
Poking me . . .
Hitting me . . .
Dragging me back,
Sitting on me,
Trapping me in his boiling prison.
He will never stop punishing me . . .
Unless I find some shade!

Harry Price (10)
Barnes Junior School

A Neglected Castle

Standing up in the pouring rain,
Wanting people to smile at him,
He sits lonely in the dark
Watching the world go by
And listening to the rattle of thunder.

He stares spookily and his mouth stays shut,
Wondering why his arms are crumbling around him,
Cobwebs stuck to his hair and skin,
He's desperate for love!

The gloomy night starts running towards him,
Trees start blowing like hurricanes,
Umbrellas turn inside out,
And he just sits cold,
Waiting . . . and waiting to be noticed.

Lucy-Rhiannon Forster (10)
Barnes Junior School

Fire

Waving my long burning arms in the air,
Whilst sharpening my long orange nails,
I stretch my hideous long legs
Until I'm tall enough to
Reach the top of your house.
Opening my mouth as wide as I can,
I give a fierce grin,
I then lash my red tongue around your house,
As tight as a clenched fist!
A gust of wind comes from my mouth
As I let a smoky cough off.
Oh no! What's this I see?
Water suddenly thrashes off my flames,
Then sadly I begin to sizzle to the ground
Whilst slowly saying goodbye!

Hannah Tullock (11)
Barnes Junior School

Snow

I'm waiting, pacing, ready to pounce,
Autumn will surrender in my frosty grasp,
I glisten in the moonlight
Providing happiness for sledgers all around.
I bring excitement to the giants below,
Falling like a child tossing a teddy out of bed.
Superstitiously I land on your window and peer in,
Watching you sit in front of the fire, cold and still.
I cuddle you with eyes of frost
Like a relative saying goodbye,
Still I force my way down,
Like a boy jumping up and down.
I'm getting tired, can't stay awake,
The burning sun, I refuse to melt.
It's time to pass for another year,
Goodbye. Oh no! I'm melting,
The spring sun wins.
I'll be back to rule again,
But it's time to die!
Goodbye!

Andrew Brewster (10)
Barnes Junior School

Autumn Leaves

Icy winds freeze my face
Like colourful helicopters,
They are crunchy like crisps in a bag.
Beautiful colours, brown, red and green
Floating like brown feathers in the sky
Leaves float down from trees
Drifting in the breeze
You can play good games with them
Kick them in the wind.

Georgia Smith (9)
Barnes Junior School

The Sun

As she rose from the horizon,
She stretched out her burning arms,
Ready to start a new day.

Sitting peacefully,
She watched over the cities,
Listening to happy children playing.

Reaching out to hug me,
So warm and so cuddly,
Just like a teddy bear,
Burning me like fire.

Brightly gleaming,
Warming up the chilly towns.
She smiles as she fades away
To sleep for the night.

Charlotte Baron 11)
Barnes Junior School

Winter

He covers the ground with his cold white carpet,
Stretching his icy fingers to make you trip over
As he crawls across the snowy, icy ground.

He watches you through
The steamy windows
That are packed with hot fires
and Christmas trees.

But when you go outside,
He blows the coldness in your face
And makes you shiver in your coat.

Then when spring finally arrives,
Sadly wailing is winter floating away.

Emily Lonsdale (11)
Barnes Junior School

My Life As A Bed

Oh here he comes, I love him but not his sister.
Oh no, his sister is here too.
Double trouble!
She's bouncing on me like a bouncy castle,
My springs are going to ache in the morning.
They're at the toilet,
It's time to run.
No, they're back.
I lost my chance to escape.
It's OK, he's alone now
And he looks sleepy.
Ooh, his warm, cosy back
Warms me up
Like a piece of toast.

Elliott Young (10)
Barnes Junior School

A Pen

It's quite boring being a pen,
Sprinting across a parchment
Day after day, after day,
Until when my user leaves me.
She carries me off to her desk
Which I call 'Home Sweet Home'.
I lay my blue head down to rest
On my owner's book.
I'm so sleepy now,
I'm just going to close my eyes.
When the sunlight starts trickling in,
I will wake up again.
Yes, I will do the same thing.
It's quite boring being a pen!

Jade Hughes (10)
Barnes Junior School

Hogwarts

I stand on a mountain
Looking over the village.
Witches and wizards climb up to me,
Clutching a burning lantern.
They enter my lips
Then I close them, so they can look around.

I am mother of the stairs
So we play all day.
Hogwarts' students often end up
Where they're not allowed,
Like Harry Potter.

I love all of the students,
They're like my children,
But some play tricks on me,
Like the Weasly twins.
I feel scared, angry, but I laugh.

I remember all their faces,
I watch them like a movie.
I've never had a holiday.

Rebecca Dewhurst (10)
Barnes Junior School

Autumn

Dry leaves crunching like
Crisps under my feet,
Bare trees shivering in the wind,
Evergreens standing like soldiers
Guarding the queen,
Leaves falling, meeting in the sky,
Bitter winds cut my face
Like a knife of frost,
Smooth conkers bashing off the ground,
Brown bushes rustling in the wind.

Lidya Balaban (8)
Barnes Junior School

Lemonade

I sit here in my ice chamber
With my cell mates.
I sit next to the mouldy cheese
And the curdled milk.
I hear a glass hit the
Hard wooden worktops.
The fridge door creaks open,
A hand grabs me.
My cell mates glare at me in envy.

I'm forcefully tipped over,
It makes me feel sick.
I'm poured, I bubble and fizz with excitement.
I think I'm going to a better place,
But am I?

Ellie Campbell (10)
Barnes Junior School

The Castle

As we creep towards the castle,
A bright light suddenly gleams,
We get closer and gaze at the fort,
With a gawping mouth
That bears razor-sharp teeth
And abandoned turrets like bushy hair.

We enter through the open door,
All three of us quivering with fear.
But as we peep through a shattered window,
We gaze upon a courtyard
With dull, crumbling arms,
But flowers like a bright Californian shirt!

Adam Johnson (10)
Barnes Junior School

The Dance Of A Paintbrush

Lying there,
Still and quiet,
On goes the light
And the dance begins.

Singing through the night like a lark,
Spinning round and round with fast feet,
Splashing and leaping through
The puddle of coloured water.

She is flung into the air,
Twirling around and around,
Finally she jumps into her washing bowl.
She pats herself dry in a warm paper towel,
Then she dances to her velvet sleeping box.

Lucy Ellis (10)
Barnes Junior School

The Grumpy Old Willow

I'm very old and lonely,
The other trees think I'm boring,
I'm bullied, ruined and bashed to bits.

Fighting to keep my balance in the bitter cold wind,
Just like a hit in the face,
My arms wave frantically and ache,
I cry and cry until it stops.

When something touches me,
I feel I've got some soul in myself . . .
But that will never happen.
I wish I wasn't the old grumpy willow anymore.

Hannah Todd (10)
Barnes Junior School

Fire

Dancing majestically on his wooden stage,
Spitting as it crackles away to ashes,
Flames waving like someone waves to their friend.

Like thunder it roars,
Burning everything in sight,
But this never lasts forever.

Running like Kelly Holmes at the Olympics,
Blazing like the sun on a summer's day,
And when it dies it is like a person at the end of their life.

Victoria Hunter (10)
Barnes Junior School

Thunder And Lightning

Like a spear stabbing from the sky,
I shoot electric arrows down to Earth.
I leap up and down in victory if I hit a tree.
When I'm bored I reach down from the clouds,
Grabbing any human I can, killing it in a cloud of smoke.
But just as I think I'm winning the battle,
The sun comes out and chases me away.

Cameron Wright (10)
Barnes Junior School

Autumn Leaves

Autumn leaves
Colourful like yellow, red, orange and brown.
Swishing in the breeze like a bee buzzing around.
Floating like a feather drifting off into sleep.
Snappy, dry like your snapping sticks.

Tiffany Eadie (8)
Barnes Junior School

Fire

He crackles like mad,
Tearing down everything in his path,
Fiercely snarling like a sly fox with a cunning plan,
His fiery flames catch alight, watching it burn to the ground.
People cry and rush about but he doesn't care!

Angrily lashing out and spreading further and further,
Laughing repeatedly at things burning and falling,
He reaches out to get you with his flickering fingers.
Heat grows stronger and very ferocious.

But just as he's getting all of his strength,
Something strikes him and he feels wet and drained.
He falls to the ground, lying alone in the night.
He's sure he will be back!

Amy Thompson (10)
Barnes Junior School

A Junk Store Chair

Crying, shifting uneasily, is a chair,
Made in Victorian time,
Complete with flares.

Sagging uncomfortably, plush velvet seat and arms,
At an extremely high price,
Many it alarms.

Dragged roughly, soft fur is on the back,
The fur's softness,
It does not lack.

Now it's in a posh home, under a portrait of a snowy-white cow.
When people come for dinner,
They always say, 'Wow!'

Sally Martin (10)
Barnes Junior School

My Life As A Bed

I walked into my bedroom
And saw my bed throwing things around
I ran to try and stop it.
Suddenly it grabbed me
And picked me up
I was slammed to the floor
Like a sack of potatoes.
I yelled 'Ouch!'
I scrambled to my feet
To my surprise
Opened my eyes
To find it was
Only a dream.

Callum Houghton (10)
Barnes Junior School

My Life As A Bed

It's night-time again.
I am all alone with the teddies,
Everything is calm.
All of a sudden, *thump, thump, thump.*
Oh no, here he comes to lie on me.
I feel as though I cannot breathe.
He tosses and turns,
I am uncomfortable.
There's a light,
It's coming through the window.
I'll be free soon.

Daniel Waugh (10)
Barnes Junior School

My Life As A Bed

The light goes on, the nightmare begins,
Oh no!
The children are coming,
Hear the children come
Who start to jump on me
And give me a bad back,
My leg starts killing me,
Mum comes upstairs and turns the light off,
They fall asleep on my body like mice,
The nightmare ends when they go to school,
I'll be lonely!
But I have my friend, the duvet
To talk to.

Sana Baber (10)
Barnes Junior School

My Life As A Bed

Here she comes,
So she can go to sleep,
She's going to take everything off me,
I'm very cold,
I don't know why she wants to get on me yet,
But she does warm me up,
I see her every day,
She doesn't hurt me,
I can hear her singing lullabies,
I can smell her brownies of lunch,
Every night the cushions tell me we're very lucky
And I believe them.

Hannah Stanger (10)
Barnes Junior School

The Young Wizard's Wand

Waiting nervously to quickly be yanked
Out from underneath the wizard's long black robes
And to be held in a warm young wizard's hand.
Yes! Excitedly I saw his hand come towards me,
Then as he picked me up my stomach turned
As he quickly pulled me out.

Laughing as I shot out stunning spells
Towards evil Dementors with their deadly look,
Spitting out spells to help, mend and move things,
I thought to myself how cool I was!

Lauren Coates (11)
Barnes Junior School

My Life As A Bed

My bed wraps its tongue around me
And keeps me snug.
I let out my feelings
My bed stores them in his mind.
Oh no! she's sitting on my head again.
I have no friends except the little old rag doll in
                                        the corner.
I say to my owner when she is asleep I need a friend I
                                        can keep.
I know I won't live in the room for much longer.

Brittany Wood (10)
Barnes Junior School

The Sahara Desert

In Africa there's a creature,
A creature named Sahara,
She's the queen of sand.
She conquers nearly half of Africa,
Suffocating trespassers in a bed of sand,
Laughing at their deaths.
She whips up storms to skin them alive
And watches them bleed to death.
Spitting up scorpions to poison them badly,
She's a torture chamber.
If you dream of death . . . go and see Sahara!

Andrew Burns (10)
Barnes Junior School

My Life As A Bed

Oh no! Those people are looking at me.
And that was the last time I saw my friends.
I was moved into the warmest room
In their house.
Jumping on me and lying on me, they celebrated.
They kept moving my mouth around
Their heads rested on my eyes
Then happiness came back when they went
away for a few weeks and I got to relax.

Kuzi Bwanya (10)
Barnes Junior School

Autumn Leaves

Cold winds make your faces numb,
Like you cannot move your face.
Autumn leaves have different colours,
Yellow is like the sun,
Brown is like a hamster,
Red is like lipstick
And orange is like an orange.
Leaves float down from trees,
Like brown feathers in the sky.
Be careful not to break them,
They are delicate you know!
They are crunchy like crisps under my feet.
I kick leaves under my feet just for fun,
With my friends having some fun.

Sacha Hawes (9)
Barnes Junior School

The Moon

In a space of my own,
Sad to say I'm not alone,
My shimmering friends love another,
As I kiss to what I call brother.
Watching him set from the sky,
I know my warriors of wolves are nearby,
Dancing, prancing, singing to me,
For I am the king bee!
So when you rest your snoozy head,
To the safe comfort of your bed,
My muscles and strengths
Are here to fight,
All throughout the silent night.

Charlotte Dunn (11)
Barnes Junior School

My Life As A Bed

One dark night he went to bed.
Oh, how my back aches from that boy.
Oh, how my legs ache all night.
I began to snap as he tossed and turned.
Near the morning he began to wake.
As he tossed and turned again
I snapped more.
He moved further down my stomach
So I tossed him up to my chest.
He woke and then got off me, I was glad.
I had the rest of the day to myself.
His mum walked into the room, I flinched . . .

Samuel James Eley (10)
Barnes Junior School

My Life As A Bed

My legs are touching the floor,
I can feel the quilt drag over me
To keep me warm.
I can feel the weight on me as
The person sits on me.
I hear chatting all around me,
I see light shining in my eyes,
I see cloth all around me,
My nose is being flattened as she
Sits on my head.
My legs are aching.

Sofenna Lowe (11)
Barnes Junior School

Autumn Leaves

Autumn leaves fall from the trees,
Swaying side to side,
Like brown feathers in the sky,
When you kick the leaves,
It sounds like snow crunching under your feet.
Cold wind cuts my face,
Like a freezing knife of frost,
That's autumn leaves.

Matthew Trimble (8)
Barnes Junior School

My Life As A Bed

What a life I have!
All day I hold many things
But my worst nightmare is
When that heavy thing doesn't have
A care in the world about me
But the most loving thing I love
Is when she makes me.

Hollie Rosborough (10)
Barnes Junior School

The Rain

The rain is a woman,
So lonely
Every window and door she passes
She lightly taps
For some lovely, caring and loyal friends.
If nobody answers her light tapping
She will move on
And look for some others
That really care for her.

Ashleigh Williamson & Rachael Dawson (11)
Bede Burn Primary School

The Hailstone And The Wind

The hailstone comes
And wets everyone in sight
He is not quiet.

For his tears are rolling down
He targets his enemy
And sieves his stones
He sets his alarm
And wakes up to dryness.

The wind sails out of the sea
And stops people in their path
Umbrellas turn inside out
And people run for shelter
She blows out and sighs
She is angry and wants to be cared for
Her friends run away from her
She has no hope left.

Chloe Parvin & Alice Carr (10)
Bede Burn Primary School

The King Of The Sky

You know when he is moving,
When he stomps like *boom!*
He rages with anger,
To scare anyone in his *room!*
He feels so confused, angry and mad,
You will not want to argue otherwise you are
Sad!

He feels so proud he thinks he is *best!*
He doesn't need to challenge,
He is better than all the *rest!*
But when he does challenge,
He does not need to try,
For he is the king of the *sky!*

Amy Farrell & Adam Curry (10)
Bede Burn Primary School

The Door

His boredom builds,
As he moans and groans,
And feels forgotten as ever,
He's trapped and lonely,
With eternities of sadness yet to come,
Like a lonely old man he gazes,
Into thin air,
Thinking of the next life he'll see,
He wonders on.

Sarah Mullin & Gabrielle Davidson (10)
Bede Burn Primary School

Autumn Sounds

A sheet of crystal is the sea so bright,
Small gems all around.
Bobbing of the boats make a lovely sound.
Blankets of green seem to appear.
Little drops of rain here and there.
Conkers popping out of their shells.
Hills covered in leaves so bright.
What colours will they be tonight?

Sarah Jane Bambrough (9)
Bede Burn Primary School

Bird's-Eye View

I can see the crystal blue ocean.
I can see the grass like crumpled paper
Splashed with green paint.
The roads are black ribbons winding everywhere.

Ross Dunn (8)
Bede Burn Primary School

A Bird's-Eye View

Soaring above in the sky,
Getting a good bird's-eye.
The crystal clear water,
Dancing below with pride.
Small boats bobbing up and down
Cliffs all round and jagged,
With small birds' nests like woven bowls,
Topped with sheets of emerald-green.
Pencil grey walls to separate every field.
A sapphire stream flows down some rocks,
Starting to come into town.
Seeing the buildings like boxes,
Hearing the bark of town foxes.
Black roads like ribbons
And a speeding train on the tracks.

Aiden Coyne (8)
Bede Burn Primary School

A Royal Family

A princess, tall and beautiful,
With a crown encrusted with gems.
She flutters her eyelashes at boys
And hopes to get a stare.
She walks with a flourish,
She has rings with diamonds on,
Which fit nicely on her slim fingers
And neatly pointed nails.
They go nicely with her pointed nails.
Her pearly-white teeth,
Go nicely with her crystal eyes,
She can really call herself a princess.

Katie Quinn (8)
Bede Burn Primary School

A Bird's-Eye View

A boat like a washed up bowl,
In the ocean with clear horses,
Swerving peacefully
And cliffs that look like
Triangular pieces of toffee.
Trees swaying from side to side like broccoli.
The sun setting down silently.
The wind whistling with faint noises.
People that look like full stops.
Cars moving along roads like fast ants.

Madeleine Brown (9)
Bede Burn Primary School

Book Action

Crocs creep, monkeys swing, lions roar.
Cheetahs dash!
Monsters scare, ghosts howl, skeletons jangle.
People run!
Jugglers juggle, acrobats flip, pies splat.
People laugh!
Ships sail, fish swim, sharks bite.
Pirates ahoy!

Harley McCourt (8)
Bede Burn Primary School

Hailstones

The clouds throw stones as fast as a cheetah runs
It's like a woodpecker pecking on your shoulder
As they rage through the sky.

Ilicia Mason & Zoe Turnbull (10)
Bede Burn Primary School

The Costume On Gran

My great gran, Primrose, came over for tea,
What a sight to see her in a tree.
'My gran Primrose only has one shoe', I said.
She has sort of candyfloss hair but she has a funny
thing to wear.
Blue, red, yellow and more, I get the feeling it's a bore.
I also feel embarrassed walking down the street with
her,
Especially in that thing she wears.
She took me to a counter and said, 'I want some tea'.
'Tell me what you want and I'll take you to your seat'.
The man gasped.
He gasped to see such a sight.
I know him from somewhere -
It's Uncle Dan! What a sight to see you in.
I think you have a chance to win.

Jackson Parker (8)
Bede Burn Primary School

The Autumn

Dew lying softly,
Wind swirling gracefully,
Birds flying south,
Berries good to eat.
TV programmes change,
Like the colour of the leaves.
Conkers crack noisily,
Squirrels gather nuts
And we're all happy together!

Amber Lea (8)
Bede Burn Primary School

The Fog

The angry dead man's spirit shuffles along
With devious eyes staring at the gloomy moon
He circles his prey
Until it can't see
Then slowly moves on
His old weepy cloak waves around him all night long
Getting caught on the branches of the trees
In the depths of the black forest
Then he followed a soaring bird to the town
Then his sadness got too great
And covered the town in his cloak.

Alice Atkinson & Jessica Birch (10)
Bede Burn Primary School

A Bird's-Eye View

Seagulls soaring in the sky,
They have a brilliant bird's-eye.
They can swoop and dive with clouds so near.
They're free as the wind, high up here.
The breeze picks up and seagulls fly.
He soars back, to his ragged nest.
He comfortably settles and dozes,
Back to sleep he goes.

Emma Gardner (9)
Bede Burn Primary School

Electricity

He soars silently through the wires,
The king of modern living must not be disturbed
Or else he can inflict a painful bite.
He will power everything if you respect him.
Be careful.

Christian Johnson-Richards & Ben Stevenson (10)
Bede Burn Primary School

The Fog

The fog moves stealthily towards it prey
A pack of wolves hungrily searching.
Its food is found.
It circles its prey
Until there's nothing but silhouettes!
The hunt is done
It moves onto the next unfortunate victim.

Ben Hall & Sophie Downie (10)
Bede Burn Primary School

The Leaves

Whipping, whirling, spinning around
And running from the wind.
Trees conducting them to stop
But they won't listen.

Running, swirling and flying around.
Wind stops,
There's not a sound.

Bethany Watkinson & Sam Drewery (10)
Bede Burn Primary School

Volcano

Once there was a lonely volcano
That had been sleeping for many years.
Someone woke me up
And I blew to the sky in force.

Adam Johnston & Jack Syrett (10)
Bede Burn Primary School

What is Snow

Snow is blinding crystals
Drifting into the deep blue sky,
Laying motionless on the frozen road.

Snow is a sparkling white angel,
Staring at the beautiful valley
That lies below.

It is a soft, furry polar bear
Searching slowly and wearily
For its prey.

Shining brightly,
It is glimmering shards of glass
Scattered upon the street.

Jonny Maddick (10)
Cragside Primary School

What Are Flowers?

Bursting into a butterfly,
Like a caterpillar from a cocoon,
Flowers blossom beautifully.

Rising like the sun,
It jumps into action,
Making the world a colourful place.

Scrunching up for wintertime,
It gradually gets smaller.

Drooping over and looking dull,
It is a dog's ear flopping over
As the curse of winter arrives.

Tamzin Anderson (11)
Cragside Primary School

What Is A Volcano?

Bursting out to the world,
A volcano is a red-hot blister
Resting on a hard, rocky foot.

A volcano is a hostile, fiery demon
burning anything in its wake.

A volcano is a man who ate too much chilli;
He sits on a burning stool of fire.

Flying faster than the speed of light,
A volcano is a gigantic, raging fire-bolt,
Locked onto its target.

A volcano is a natural flamethrower,
Burning nature and other life without regret.

Alexander Martin (10)
Cragside Primary School

What Is Snow?

Snow is a soft, furry polar bear,
Searching wearily for somewhere to sleep.

Snow is a beautiful white angel
Sitting majestically on a soft cloud.

Snow is a soft white blanket
Spreading over the valley.

It is icing sugar softly sprinkled
From the clear blue sky.

Snow is little balls of fluffy wool
Falling to the frozen ground.

Lauren Short (10)
Cragside Primary School

What Are Flowers?

Exploding into millions of beautiful scents,
The flower bursts into a colourful butterfly
Swaying up into the blue, never-ending sky,
Landing gently on a pretty pale pink rose.

The flower is a pretty little girl, digging herself into the soil,
Dancing to the music that lays beyond the world
Sinking into the quicksand.
The flower grabs hold of a nearby friend.

Flowers are like small raindrops
Sprinkled onto the hard ground,
Bending cheerfully down
To tickle your toes.

Aisha Khan (10)
Cragside Primary School

What Is the Moon?

The moon is a silver ten pence piece
Drifting across the sky without a care in the world.
Magically glistening away behind the gusty trees,
The moon is a glossy crystal.
It is a polished whiteboard, a smooth glittering star,
Painting the sky with magical moonlight.
Shining luminously in the distance, it is
A satin sun painted with glistening white paint.
Glowing with light, the moon is an eerie white ship
Floating away like a ghostly galleon.
The moon is a sparkling white pearl gleaming with delight.
Flashing in the midnight sky,
The moon is a light bulb guiding weary travellers.

Laura Phillips (10)
Cragside Primary School

What Is A Hurricane?

Hurtling down from the hands
Of a raging man to its court
Of destruction, a hurricane is
A Beyblade sprinting at its enemy.

A hurricane is an evil wizard in his lair
Stirring up his darkest spells.

A hurricane is God's cup of black coffee
Whirling with all its might.

Galloping hastily whilst being whipped
By its owner, stamping on anything
In its track, a hurricane is
A horse jumping over any hurdles.

Ryan Holmes (10)
Cragside Primary School

What Are Icicles?

Icicles are frozen fingers,
Crooked and jagged.

Piercing through delicate skin,
Icicles are sharp and dangerous daggers.

They are sharks' teeth, lethal weapons
As they fall to the ground.

Dazzling in the sunlight,
Icicles are shimmering crystals.

Icicles are fingernails scratching
My smooth and soft hands.

Nicole Kortenbach (10)
Cragside Primary School

What Is The Solar System?

The solar system is a
Gigantic black wasted space,
Unused and unwanted.

The solar system is
A huge adventure
Waiting to be unfolded.

The solar system is a
Magician's cape filled with
Magic fairy dust gleaming
In the sun's elegant rays.

Swallowing all those
Who dare to enter,
The solar system is a sandstorm
In a black night desert.

Scattering silvery stars
In a pitch-black sky,
The solar system is
Colossal!

Amy Topping (10)
Cragside Primary School

Wide Open

W e score all the goals
I n the back of the net
D o all the tackling
E nough to win the league

O range and blue are our arch enemies
P enalties and free kicks we don't need
E ven though we have been beaten
N obody can beat us now.

Ben Sutton (9)
Greenfields Community Primary School

Come And Stay for The Night

Come and stay at the haunted house
As witches fly around the chamber.

The church has been here,
You live very near

So don't disturb the dead.
Every Christmas you have dinner here

And we will make you
Thinner and thinner

Until you're in your grave, so be brave,
Come into the haunted house.

As you take a peek,
Don't be so sweet

Cos they will grab you then they
Will stab you, so escape as you can.

So come into the haunted house
And come and stay the night!

Dionne Robson (9)
Greenfields Community Primary School

Wide Open

We are champions, we don't let any goals get in.
It is wise that we don't let any goals in.
Did we win at Blackpool? No we didn't,
But we are still as good as the winners.
Eagles they call us because we are fast.
Open spaces we can see
But please let us on, we say,
Else we will quit the team.
Now we are third we go mad,
But we get beaten by Graingerpark Dragons.

James Crooks (10)
Greenfields Community Primary School

December

Jumping on heaps of snow like a big marshmallow,
Listening to the radio,
Christmas soon, can't wait.
Tree is up but not too late!
Four days to go, so soon,
But I can't wait any longer.
One day to go,
Desperate for all my presents.
My brother, mum and dad can't wait,
Just like me.
Surprise tomorrow, so excited,
Bed now, can't wait.
25th of December,
Christmas never better.
All my toys and brother's gum,
Go upstairs so I can pinch some!

Ellie Glover (9)
Greenfields Community Primary School

Autumn Days

Autumn days when the leaves fall off the trees,
When the trees let them all free.
You walk on them as they crunch and they
Huddle in a bunch.
And the pretty leaves shine red, yellow and gold.
Autumn days when the trees fall plain
And you get wet in the soggy rain.
You turn on the fire and are cosy on the inside.
And the pretty leaves shine red, yellow and gold.
Autumn days when the trees let off their leaves.
But that is the season that leaves lots of bare trees.
In foggy winds they jump about.
And the pretty leaves shine red, yellow and gold.

Daniel Ferguson (9)
Greenfields Community Primary School

I Saw A Tree

I saw a tree,
Yes I saw a tree
In the middle of the forest.
It gleamed at me
With its red shiny bark
And its black and brown leaves.
I saw a tree that gleamed at me!

I saw a tree,
Yes I saw a tree,
And when I touched it
My hand shivered
Like a frozen breeze.
I saw a tree,
Yes I saw a tree
And when I turned away it gleamed at me!

Hannah Black (9)
Greenfields Community Primary School

Christmas

Christmas Eve, time to wait,
Till the morning just can't wait.
Get to bed my mum said, or
Santa will not come again.

Christmas Day, time to play,
Wake my dad up for this day.
Coming down I hear the clock
Chiming for nine o'clock.
My mum comes down in her frock,
Looking like a peacock.
Everyone down, now time to open
All my presents on Christmas Day.

Abigail Cook (9)
Greenfields Community Primary School

Autumn Covered Forest

I walked into the forest and sat down on the riverbank.
I looked round and saw tall, tall oak trees surrounding me.
I saw beautiful gold leaves flip along the dusty path.
I saw a gorgeous rabbit hop through a berry bush.

I heard the stream flow around huge rocks.
I heard the bluebirds chirping in the trees.
I heard hopping frogs croak.
I heard leaves crackling softly.

I felt a cool breeze blow through my hair.
I felt the bitter cold water tickle my toes.
I felt a small rabbit come up and rub my fingers.
I felt rough bark on my right.
And then I left the fabulous forest.

Megan Raffle (9)
Greenfields Community Primary School

Houghton Boys

H appy people when you score
O n the bench or on the pitch
U p they jump
G o on, cheer your team on
H uddle up and make a plan
T o the pitch
O ther team winning 2-1
N ever been beaten

B oys, we need to win
O n the pitch you need to score
Y es, we win
S o here's the cup.

Matthew O'Donnell (9)
Greenfields Community Primary School

Haunted House

It stood before me, the big old house
Under a bright full moon I heard a wolf
Somewhere nearby
But I'm not scared
The door creaked open without me pushing
And inside there was no life (so I thought)
But I'm not scared
I lit the torch and walked down the hall
And saw a staircase before me
But I'm not scared
Each stair made a noise like my grandfather
Snoring as I walked up and up
But I'm not scared
I got to the top and another door opened itself
But I'm not scared
I walked inside and there was an old wooden chest
But I'm not scared
As I reached for the chest I woke
But I wasn't in bed I was in an old wooden chest
And someone was scrabbling at the latch . . .

Charlotte Anderson (9)
Greenfields Community Primary School

I Saw A Spider

I saw a spider with a silver body.
I saw a blue web gleaming in the dark.
I saw a fly trapped in a web.
I heard a rat creep around the floorboards.
I saw a ghost swallow up a whale.

Andrew Armstrong (9)
Greenfields Community Primary School

Light

Light is a bold hero
Rescuing me from darkness
It doesn't make me feel like zero.

Light helps me see things
Like flowers and cars
It feels like my feet are springs.

Light battles the evil darkness
Winning every time
Tidying the blood-splattered mess.

Light embarrassingly reveals
My untidy room like a bomb dropped
As I scuttled around the room and hurt my heels.

Light is as bright
As the sun
There is no limit to its height.

Light is my best friend
It's always bright
I hope it will never end.

Liam Butler (11)
John F Kennedy Primary School

Laughter

Laughter is when someone laughs all the way
Through a film when it is not even funny.

Laughter is where someone screws up
In a lesson at school.

Laughter is Tommy the Trumpeter
And getting up and playing golf games.

Laughter is singing
And dancing on the karaoke.

Jasmine Charlton (10)
John F Kennedy Primary School

Jealously

Jealously is a bitter enemy
I feel him creep on me
He makes me envy
It's like a door with no key.

He wears green
He moves very gently
And he mostly picks on teens
I hate jealously.

He is a starving tiger
With no other friends
He is a good fighter
It's like a field with no fence.

He picks on me
When my sister's around
She spills tea
And laughs like a clown.

Aryan Sheikhalian (10)
John F Kennedy Primary School

Shyness

Shyness crept silently towards me
In a corner of the playground
Trapping me like its prisoner.

I tried to send it away
But it wouldn't let me;
It wouldn't budge.

It's keeping me back
In ropes so I can't do what I want
And holding me back from the group.

Shyness is a wall building, higher
And blocking me from the world.

Chloe Ross (10)
John F Kennedy Primary School

Fun!

Fun snooping around under the tracks
Jumping out at children.
Fun bursting out from nowhere
Putting a smile on people's faces.
Children laughing and screaming
As the roller coaster zooms past.
Children twirling and whirling
As the merry-go-round twists around.
The theme park is full of happy faces
And the sound of laughter.
As the sun goes down over the horizon
With a smile on its face
Happy people leave the park.
When the park is closed
Fun moves on somewhere else.
Where do you think fun will strike next?

Matthew Softley (10)
John F Kennedy Primary School

Fear

Fear is the wind creeping on the car,
Telling him about the rock that can fall on him,
The car is getting worried about it and wants to go the bar.

Fear makes it go zooming,
With the driver being selfish,
The mountain crashing onto the car fuming.

Fear is what the driver can't feel
Being stupid and speeding,
Trying to get away to steal.

Fear is sly,
Blowing rocks onto a car,
It's too late it crashed, bye-bye.

Jordan Taylor (10)
John F Kennedy Primary School

Fear

Fear's pale face lit up
As he saw children with fun,
His enemy.
The children laughed and giggled on,
Where fear just moved along.

He whispered in their little ears,
'Don't go on this ride, there'll be even more tears.'
The children gulped in fright,
'Are you going on?'
'I might.'

They stood in silence, also still.
They remembered the picture
Of the scary roller coaster,
On Mum's window sill.

They walked away from fear,
He smirked.

Abbie Dixon (10)
John F Kennedy Primary School

The Lion

The lion proudly roars in the morning
As he shakes his golden mane at the sun.
The lion pounces into the shining lake
Licking his paw.

The lion eats his prey
As he happily brushes his fur in the warm breeze.
The lion eats his prey
As night begins to appear.

The lion sleeps in a rocky wet cave
Underneath the grey gloomy mountains
Near by the savannah river trickling past the cave
It was another day ahead of him.

Alex Boylen (10)
John F Kennedy Primary School

Laughter

Laughter, lively shouts
To the group of kids
Pulling off their bottle lids
To come and have fun with him.

Laughter, as noisy as a bunch of girls
Screams and giggles
While he fiddles
At the children.

Laughter excitedly jumped into the young child
She started to dance!
Soon after she started to prance!
While her friends were laughing.

Laughter was noisily telling jokes
Bouncing up and down
In the middle of town
To the bunch of giggling girls.

Laughter talking nicely began to sing
To his friends and family
'By the way my name is Stanley
And I would like to say *goodbye!*'

Hannah McKinlay (10)
John F Kennedy Primary School

Confusion

The boy was working motionless.
Confusion crept stealthily up to the boy.
Confusion whispered, 'What does this mean, what on earth?'
Confusion scratched his head.

Confusion pulled a face.
Confusion whispered, 'Eh?'
The boy was now confused.
So, if you're ever confused, that's how it happens.

Daniel Craigs (10)
John F Kennedy Primary School

Young Writers - Little Laureates Poems From Tyne & Wear

The Theme Park

Fun waves and screams,
As they arrive
Eating ice cream!

Fun stupidly jumped on the cart,
Of the roller coaster
Grinning, ready to start!

Fun shouts at its friends,
Lively as a gorilla
As he pretends!

Fun quickly played naughty tricks
To get to the front of the queue of the swings
To fly on its wings!

Fun waves and screamed
Like a silly old bat
As he dreamed.

Emma Noble (10)
John F Kennedy Primary School

The Car Ride

Fear whispered scarily
Into the children's ear
As quiet as a mouse.

Fear crept past the car ride
Rolling his eyes at the car
Pointing at the children.

Fear was a shadow
As he snuck past the parents
Into the seat behind the children.

Fear, sly as a fox
Tapped the children with his old wooden stick
And grinned at them.

Emma Dover (10)
John F Kennedy Primary School

The Cave!

Darkness can be
As big as a house
Or as small as a mouse.

Darkness crept into the cave
Hitting his wooden stick
Scaring the cavemen.

Darkness prodded the caveman's shoulder
With his white hands
When the caveman was looking around.

Darkness nudged
The terrified people
While he was sliding past.

Darkness fades away
When the sun comes
At the break of the day!

Emily Marriner (10)
John F Kennedy Primary School

Happiness

Happiness
Is a hot sunny day
Getting excited and stupid.

Happiness
Is doing cartwheels on
A shiny green grass.

Happiness
Is doing roly-polys down
The hill on the field.

Happiness
Is skipping along paths
And licking ice lollies on a hot day.

Holly Rawson (10)
John F Kennedy Primary School

Fear

Fear sneaked
Around the child's bedroom,
Staring at her.

Fear
As quiet as a mouse,
Jumped out at the children.

Fear quietly talked
To the child about his fears,
He was as sly as a fox.

Fear silently ran
After the children,
Making them sprint away,
Screaming!

Thea McMullan-Jones (10)
John F Kennedy Primary School

Fun At School

Fun happily ran
Through the classroom
Disturbing the children with a toy lamb.

Fun naughtily tapped
On the classroom door
Trying to be funny.

Fun stupidly threw
Food across the cafeteria
Starting a food fight with his crew.

Fun sprinted through the school
As mad as a hatter
Causing as much trouble as possible.

Matthew Wylie (11)
John F Kennedy Primary School

Fun

Fun zoomed past
The sad people
And cheered them up.

Fun screamed
All the way through
The roller coaster ride
When it was really slow.

Fun laughed
As he was standing
In the queue for ice cream.

Fun sat
With a smile on his face
All through the funeral!

Jamie Natton (10)
John F Kennedy Primary School

Darkness

Darkness is a monster,
Creeping by,
Like a shadow creeping by.

Darkness is under the bed,
Screeching like a bat,
Ready to scare.

Darkness is a lamp turning off in the bedroom,
Monsters that creep upon you,
Hiding in the wardrobes.

Darkness is the moon coming up,
When the door slams with the wind,
And werewolves come.

Oliver Manley (10)
John F Kennedy Primary School

Fun

Fun scampered
Through the theme park
Staring at children,
Having a good time,
Fun giggled at the children.

Fun tapped
Children on the shoulder,
Putting them off
The car game.

Fun pushed
Its way through the unhappy crowd,
Turning them happy,
Making them laugh like hyenas!

Fun roared
As it went down the bank
On a roller coaster
As it loop-the-looped.

Aaron Monaghan (10)
John F Kennedy Primary School

Fear

Waiting impatiently, the children
Moaned in the long line.
Creeping slowly up to the excited children,
Fear grabbed their attention.

Talking quietly fear scared the children,
Whilst waiting in line.
The children scattered as fear
Laughed watching them struggle.

Jamie Drysdale (10)
John F Kennedy Primary School

It's Just Fear

Waiting, excitedly at the roller coaster,
Laughing at other people,
Three children stood.
Menacingly,
Fear snuck up on the satisfied children.
Sun shone down
On the ground with burning arrows.
Petrifyingly,
Fear shocked all the fidgeting children.
Fear was so frightening,
He scared the sun, the birds, the clouds
And all the other people.
The bright sun, the playful children,
The white fluffy clouds
And the chirping birds all fled.
Fear had done what he wanted to!

Alexander Cotterill (10)
John F Kennedy Primary School

Fear!

The unnoticed fear pursued
The children waiting in line
For the roller coaster.

Fear snuck up behind them
And slowly ruffled their hair
Like soft fur.

Fear menacingly whispered
In their ears,
'That roller coaster looks scary like me!'.

The children whirled
Around to see nothing . . .
But fear creeping into the darkness.

John Petersen (11)
John F Kennedy Primary School

Love!

Love falls from the sky like snow,
It falls quite low.

The sun pushes the heavy rain cloud away,
It'll come back another day.

Love hugs and blows kisses to people in love,
It is sent from above.

Birds flutter down singing and dancing,
I hope they don't come prancing.

Some girls fall in love with frogs,
That sit on logs.

From Earth to Saturn,
Love is found in Latin.

Sally Charlton (10)
John F Kennedy Primary School

Fun

Fun silently crept up
On the unsuspecting children
Fun tickled
The young sad children.

The young children
Were being filled
With laughter.

The sun shone
Like a bright fireball.
The ball bounced over fun.
Fun ran off in pursuit
Of more laughter.

Curtis Borthwick (10)
John F Kennedy Primary School

Fear

Children chattering waiting for turns
Talking about many things, but they needed to learn
That fear creeps up on you.
Fear had found them, he was whispering slyly.
The children panicked,
They heard the terrible muttering of fear.
Fear left smirking and laughing.
Children making a big fuss.
Running as fast as they could
Fear following them wherever they went!

Adam Miskell (10)
John F Kennedy Primary School

Sadness

Sadness hits the girls' friendship and shatters into a million pieces.
As she was sorted out sadness rumbled and moaned.
Determined to make friends,
Not sure to make up.
Every moment sadness appeared and made her think again.
Silence strikes but lost its taste.
Sadness says goodbye till next time.

Sophie Maughan (10)
John F Kennedy Primary School

Hunger

As the cake came out of the oven the children got more tense.
Slowly hunger snatched the cake away.
Slyly, hunger teased the children with the cake.
Unexpectedly, hunger scoffed down the cake.
After the cake was eaten
The three children went off in a huff.

Corey Butters (10)
John F Kennedy Primary School

Fun

Singing and giggling fun danced,
Up to the bored children,
Who were sitting in the corner.

Slowly the barbecue was burning
And the sun glittering,
Fun tried to make the children laugh,
By tickling their toes with a feather.

With the beautiful weather
And the yellow feather,
Fun finally made the children laugh.

Clowning around,
The children laughed and joked
With fun.

The sun went behind a fluffy cloud,
The music stopped,
Fun disappeared
And the party was over.

Emma Wylie (11)
John F Kennedy Primary School

Fun

Cheerfully, fun skipped onto the dance floor
In front of the miserable children.
The children stood in a world of misery.
Fun tried so hard to cheer the children up
He burst into laughter at his own jokes.
Suddenly, the children's faces lit up in delight.
They jumped, twisted and danced, danced, danced
Until the break of day.
Fun and his new friends were so tired
They dropped on the dance floor
And slept for the rest of the day.

Sarah Smith (10)
John F Kennedy Primary School

Love

Love affectionately
Crept into the
Room.

Love turned round
And came into
Sight.

Love combined
Two delighted people
Together.

Love laughed
And made happiness
Between them.

Love watched
As they kissed
Goodbye.

Love left
Leaving people
In their hearts.

Georgia Robison (10)
John F Kennedy Primary School

The Emotional River

The river cries down the mountains
And over the waterfalls
Until it cries itself to sleep.

Now the river is sleeping through the meanders,
While the fish are sprinting to the open sea,
To meet their long-lost family.

When the river opens his mouth
So gracefully the fish and the river
Spread into the open sea.

Joe Wilson (11)
Kingston Park Primary School

The Rushing River

River dives swiftly from his sacred source,
Never falling off course.
He swims downstream,
His eyes gleam,
He passes through the forest.

Land evens out,
He has no doubt.
He'll get there before the rest!
He giggles all the way.
Round the meander it goes,
Where only he knows.

He's done it!
He can feel it,
He's going for the gold!
He opens his mouth and greets the ocean,
Friends to the end.

Bethanie Culyer (11)
Kingston Park Primary School

The River

River trickling down the mountain
Gushing and bubbling like a baby
Gulping anything in its way
Twirling and dancing through the day.

Merrily meandering round the bends
Still gasping for air.
Spinning boulders like a whirlwind
Wearing away the river bed.

The river sprinting soon calmed down
Turned into a delta-like hand
Showing love and affection
For the glittering sea at last.

Hannah Pyle (11)
Kingston Park Primary School

The River

Roaring river
In a hurry.
Tumbling waterfall,
Starting to cry.

Scrambling streams,
Trying to catch up.
Angry eddies
Frothing and swirling.

Slowing down
And starting to laugh.
Kicking stones
And eating more land.

Almost at the salty world,
He gargles with glee
And stretches right out
To greet the deep blue sea.

Emily Brown (10)
Kingston Park Primary School

The River!

The river roars
As the rocks
Come stumbling down
With anger.

The river flows
Down a rocky mountain
As they reach the gentle waterfall.

As the river meanders
Round with glee
It just about reaches
The sea . . .

Lois Mason (10)
Kingston Park Primary School

The Running River

The waterfall was rushing,
Racing down the stream,
Gushing through the rocks,
Anger.

Joyfully jogging, swirling and twirling,
Meandering merrily, giggling and smiling,
Dancing for the glowing sun,
Chuckling.

Tears dripping into the sea,
Calmly flowing, crying and sighing,
Drooping and dropping, going to sleep,
Crying.

Beth Lant (10)
Kingston Park Primary School

The River

Charging down the mountain,
Trailing twigs and grasping rocks,
I will not stop.

Stroking the soft leaves,
The tears glittering in the sun,
Must go on.

Slowly dragging myself,
Gently meandering,
Finally.

The foam dancing like sprites,
Colours spreading into a rainbow,
I am home.

Honor Corfield (10)
Kingston Park Primary School

The Rapid River

The river was running down the mountain
Ever so quickly to meet its friend.
The river was lazily meandering round the corners,
Tumbling over the stones
Stealing everything in its way.

The river's rapidly growing current
Strongly pulling rocks to the river bed.
River bank eroding terribly
On its journey to the sea.

The river running, skipping over stones
Then jumping youthfully
Splitting into a valley
Overlapping everything in its path.

Brandon Cooper (10)
Kingston Park Primary School

Rushing River

Rushing river is as fierce as
A killer chasing its prey.
It sprints through its path
Down the raging river.

It wraps the rough rocks
In its gushing waters.
It rapidly rips the rocks apart
As it rumbles down the mountains.

Reece Havelock-Brown (10)
Kingston Park Primary School

The River's Last Laugh

Shouts and screams of the fearless stream,
As he rips apart the riverbank.
He brings out his claws,
Tossing and tumbling as he begins to fight thunder.

Winning his battle, he feels unstoppable,
As he chuckles downstream.
He strums at the hillside,
His very own guitar,
A huge pioneer's heart.

He pushes aside the rocky coastline,
Like slicing through a dense jungle.
Then he starts to cry,
His life at an end,
As he becomes the next victim of the sea.

Amy Dalrymple (11)
Kingston Park Primary School

The River

The river is zooming down the waterfall
And crashing on the rocks.
The river is jogging along on its winding path.
Flooding the grassy banks.
Chuckling over the riverbank.
Spreading its way like a hand.
Fingers streaming along to the sea.
Floating off mixing in the sea.

Jack Robson (10)
Kingston Park Primary School

River

Stumbling down the mountain's face,
The stream is very fierce.
Clasping anything in his grasp,
To take on his journey to the glittering sea.

After throwing itself into a stunning waterfall,
I could only watch and stare,
To see the stream slow right down,
Laughing as he turned into a river.

Sprinting as he opens his mouth,
He meets his friend the sea.
His smile gleaming as he turns into,
His best friend the glittering sea!

Rebecca Henry (11)
Kingston Park Primary School

The Racing River

The river was roaring furiously,
It was sprinting with anger,
From mountain to mountain,
Stealing rocks and pebbles.

It was laughing evily by waterfalls,
He wants to be,
The first to reach
Its beloved sea . . .

The river is now stretching,
To relax in the sea,
He is joyful!

Reema Albalushi (10)
Kingston Park Primary School

My First Show

My first show, first stage,
Feeling scared, all alone.
Dancing and singing with
A bit of drama.

My first show,
The lights flashing.
The Wizard of Oz,
Was about to begin.

The magical feeling,
Running around the stage, dancing,
This really was the Wizard of Oz.

Paradise was over, this was it,
My make-up done,
My costume was on.

My first show,
The lights were flashing,
The Wizard of Oz had started.

The people clapping, witches and fairies flying
Into the sky.
Dancers dancing, singers singing,
It was magical.

The show was nearly over,
No more magical shows
'Til next year or maybe next week.

My first show,
The Wizard of Oz, was over.

Hannah Hailes (10)
Marley Hill Community Primary School

It's Not Just Me

I was on my own 'til 2005.
That year a surprise came,
A very, very, very big surprise.

I was on my own
I was on my own
I was on my own
. . . 'til . . .

The thing came along
That thing was a little girl called Zoe.
A little girl that screamed,
Cried, slept and ate.

I'm not by myself
I'm not by myself
I'm not by myself
. . . Anymore . . .

Then she turned 1,
In 2006, 5th of December
She was really funny then,
. . .Until . . .

We'll stick together
We'll stick together
We'll stick together
. . . Forever . . .

2007 came
It was a rough year for my mum,
Zoe running about.
Me, well she didn't have to worry then.

There's something coming
There's something coming
There's something coming
. . .There is . . .

It was another thing
The exact same
This one was called Brooke.
She screams, cries, eats and sleeps.

We'll all stick together
We'll all stick together
We'll all stick together
. . . Now . . .

Kelsey Madden (10)
Marley Hill Community Primary School

The Sea Aquarium

Once we went to Tynemouth.
When we were there, we went to the aquarium.

Once we were inside, my dad said
We could go and see the turtle display,
Inside the aquarium.

When we were inside the sea tunnel,
There were rays, to crabs, to jellyfish,
Inside the aquarium.

When we came to the giant squid,
It was catching its prey,
Inside the aquarium.

Then we saw the king crab, it was huge,
So huge it could eat a cat,
Inside the aquarium.

It was crab holding time, they had millions,
But I only had time to hold two,
Inside the aquarium.

After that we saw sharks.
There were reef sharks to bottom sharks,
Inside the aquarium.

Mathew Wilson (10)
Marley Hill Community Primary School

My Little Pony

My little pony
Got him two years ago.
My little pony
Loved him like a baby.
My little pony
Kept him in a stable.
My little pony
Fed every morning.
My little pony
Hugged every morning.
My little pony
Loved every day
And night.
My little pony
Chose him at morning.
My little pony
Rode him around.
My little pony
Got him from a stable yard.
My little pony
Got a rosette.
My strong winning little pony
Is a star!

Elissa Mennell (11)
Marley Hill Community Primary School

I Can Swim!

Mrs Raye called my name,
In the pool I went.
Would I sink?
Would I drown?
Butterflies in my stomach,
I pushed off.
Would I sink?
Would I drown?
After a metre I stopped.
Could I go on? Yes I could, yes I could,
I didn't sink.
I didn't drown.
I had done it,
I really had.
I'll never sink,
I'll never drown.
Now I always want to go swimming!

Bethany Lowes (10)
Marley Hill Community Primary School

Big Tall Man

Cheering like a crowd,
Upon the night rocks,
Never been so proud,
He always takes his bows,
To the dark night owls,
His light begins to dim,
As the sun comes up,
He sighs and sleep sets in.

Brian Quinn (11)
New Penshaw Primary School

Differences

Ivy Rose is a tall rich lady,
With sparkling eyes and white, white teeth,
Her pearl dress shimmers in the sun,
As she looks at her surroundings and sighs,
As she is spoilt with a new bright coat,
Her beads shake in the wind,
Blue, purple, yellow and red,
Are her beads wrapped round her head.

Number 15, poor old man,
With holes in his hat and cuts on his head,
The little old man shakes in the bitter wind,
As time ticks by his friends are dead,
Over the road are the big rich men with big top hats,
They've ordered the bulldozer to get rid of the scruffy old man,
1 . . . 2 . . . 3 . . . and now he is dead
They cheer, they sing, they clap - hooray for now he is gone!

Chloe Bellas (11)
New Penshaw Primary School

The Big Old Man

Number 11, the big old man,
Standing tall on the hillside,
Watching his company go by,
His only friends are the big old birds,
Who want to play every day
Up on his hat and his spiky hair,
In the cold he wears his thick white coat,
With eyes so shiny and bright,
As he smokes his big old cigar
Being surrounded by water,
It's a shame he cannot swim,
So he's here forever up on the hill.

Ryan Hamilton (10)
New Penshaw Primary School

The Lonely Soul

Number 15 is a lonely old soul, kindly and shy,
He cannot see the dead flowers that lie nearby,
With no one around him to bother or care,
He has no friends - he has no pair,
Yet he hasn't realised life often passes,
Until he looks through the cracks in his old grey glasses,
Seeing mice that scurry, scamper and hide,
Bringing a ray of sunshine, a hint of pride,
There up on the wood - he feels less lonely,
Now he knows he has friends to keep him company.

Sharn Hannan (11)
New Penshaw Primary School

The Mansion

The big old man standing proudly on the hill,
Wearing his white coat adorned with gold trim,
Surrounded by water it's a shame he can't swim,
The sun reflects on his huge glasses,
He often looks lonely as no one passes,
But the sweet sound of birds keeps him company,
As he passes the day standing so proudly.

Nathan Wilson (10) & Callum Genther (10)
New Penshaw Primary School

Old Lady

Number 13 is an old craggy woman,
With broken lenses and a dry red mouth,
With her old-fashioned make-up, blue and white,
Sitting on the bumpy green floor she's really tall.

Natasha Raymond (10)
New Penshaw Primary School

The Island

Number 1, a big old rich man,
Wearing his grey suit,
He shimmers with glee,
Smoking his cigar,
With his crown on his head.

Number 2, a short old woman,
With lovely black hair,
The sun shines on her glasses,
Wearing her white jacket,
With an apple tree to keep her company.

Next door is her husband,
A tall old man,
Wearing his knitted red and white jumper,
Up all night shining his torch,
Seagulls nest on his top hat.

Nathan Hutchinson (11)
New Penshaw Primary School

Sunderland Man

His big yellow eyes go constantly around,
Wearing his bright Sunderland top,
Shouting to boats beware the danger,
With his grey stone hat seen from afar.

Dead at morning as his light goes out,
Seagulls cheering like a crowd,
Seeing if any boats are still about,
Upon his black rocks, never has rowed.

Bedded upon the old rock,
Lonely souls above him,
Sitting next to the docks,
His bright light goes dim.

Regan Naisbett (10)
New Penshaw Primary School

The Twins And The Big Old Man

Number 11 and 10, two twins sitting together,
With their dusty old faces and their shining eyes
Playing happily, sharing their sun hat together,
And picking at their sky with their tall hands.

Number 11, the big old man standing tall,
His huge open mouth, waiting for friends to arrive,
On the hillside waiting for the knock,
The birds keeping him company each day alive.

Kieron Hughes (10)
New Penshaw Primary School

The Big Rich Man

A big old rich man,
Wearing his drab grey suit.
He shimmers with glee.
Smoking his big cigar,
With his tall pointed hat,
He smiles as the day goes on,
And every day the sun passes.

Billy Davison (11)
New Penshaw Primary School

The Lighthouse

Tall old man,
Standing on the rocks,
Beaming his torch out across the high seas,
With his Sunderland strip on,
He makes sure boats don't crash,
Until morning comes, lights go out.

Kenya Allen (11)
New Penshaw Primary School

The Mansions

The big fat man number 5,
Stood there alone,
With his big gold jacket,
And an ice cream cone
Flew in his mouth,
Surrounded by water
Too bad he can't swim,
Just standing there alone!
With his shiny glasses,
Just standing there,
With a path right in front,
And a tall pointed hat,
And then it turns white
When the moon comes out.

Number 1 a big tall boy,
With shiny bright beads,
And big squared eyes,
Watching people passing by,
When he stands there alone,
And a big top hat,
With a flower on the top,
And then someone adopts him
Before he was alone,
With his top hat on,
And now he is at home.

Dominic Turnbull (11)
New Penshaw Primary School

Tall And Narrow

Number 13 is a stressed young girl,
With broken lenses and a cracked grin,
Her lovely make-up, all yellow and purple,
Surrounded by pretty bright beads,
Gleaming brightly in the morning sun,
She sits so house proud upon the old hill.

Kim Mason (11)
New Penshaw Primary School

Street

Ivy Rose is a rich young lady,
With sparkling teeth and gleaming eyes,
Her lovely pearl dress shimmers in the sun,
With crystal clear water out to her front,
She looks at herself and sighs!
Across the road is . . .
Number 7, a big fat man,
Standing tall and proud,
With his head up in the cloud,
No family, no friends, he's all alone!

Abby Johnson (10)
New Penshaw Primary School

The Forest

The big fat old man standing with pride,
Wearing his black pinstriped suit,
With a tall and narrow top hat,
With his broken spectacles like shattered ice,
Surrounded by trees, a shame he can't walk,
With him all alone, only the birds as his friends,
The blowing wind makes him scream his name,
As the birds circle him twenty-four seven.

Chloe Poulter (10)
New Penshaw Primary School

Two Strong Twins

Number 9 and 11, the similar twins,
Sitting and sighing in the strong winds,
Sitting there as tough as a bus,
While all the people stand there and fuss,
As the twins compete with each other,
They argue over who's the best brother!

Eddy Burney (10)
New Penshaw Primary School

My Mansions

Number 9 - a very old lady,
She sits in the long green grass,
Her silky rags are overgrown,
She wishes that people would love her.

Number 10 - a very elderly man,
The wind whistles like a howling wolf,
Through the holes in his old top hat,
Standing all alone in the pouring rain,
His only friend - a very old cat.

Caitlin Vest (10)
New Penshaw Primary School

Number 15

Number 15 is a lonely old bloke,
The wind blows his black and white cap,
His big cigar leaves a trail of smoke,
From afar it looks like he's having a nap,
As the rain hits his dull old glasses,
With his bony hands pointing to home,
Nobody ever bothers or passes,
Leaving him sleeping on the grass all alone.

Jack Ramsden (11)
New Penshaw Primary School

Mansion Man

Number 15 is a proud fat man,
He sits there with an orange tan,
His bright blue eyes sparkle away,
He stops there still - day by day,
He has a big weird hat upon his head,
At night he sleeps on his big green bed.

Nathan McMenam (11)
New Penshaw Primary School

All Alone

Number 12 all alone waits for someone to talk to,
Tears dripping down his sad old face,
When the wind blows his mouth flaps wide,
Then he realises there is nobody to care,
There never will be as he approaches his deathbed,
Then his legs ache and now he is dead.

Number 26 standing on the rocks,
Beaming his torch out to the seas,
With his proud Sunderland top on,
Making sure boats don't crash,
When morning comes his light goes off,
Until dusk arrives like the candle going out,
When his endless watch begins all over again.

Roseann Galloway (11)
New Penshaw Primary School

The Spooky Haunted Mansions

The old man sitting alone,
With his smashed and scratched glasses,
With his mouth about to fall off,
And his hat with thousands of holes inside,
Sitting on that hill all day, silent!

A crying old man,
Sitting in the woods all alone,
Holes through his flat pointy hat,
Cracks through all of his body
All alone on a grassy green hill.

Michael Layford (11)
New Penshaw Primary School

The Dragon Who Ate Our Farm

When she came to the farm
First she sat on the barn
She squashed the horses
So they couldn't do their courses.

She's a beautiful colour
But you mustn't go near her
Otherwise she'll gobble you up!

She ate the sheep
She kicked them
And they landed in a heap.

She's a beautiful colour
But you mustn't go near her
Otherwise she'll gobble you up!

Then she gobbled up a lamb
And chased my auntie Pam.

She's a beautiful colour
But you mustn't go near her
Otherwise she'll gobble you up!

I ran towards a wall
The gap was very small
I squashed through the gap
But the dragon was trapped.

She's a beautiful colour
But you mustn't go near her
Otherwise she'll gobble you up!

Morgan Whitaker (7)
New York Primary School

My Perfect World

No vandalism
Perfect garden
No dog poo
Lovely swimming pool
No glass
Fabulous furniture
No graffiti

My perfect world

Perfect house
No staying in at playtime
Bouncy bed
No robbers, definitely not
Loads of skate parks
Never getting grounded
Lots of pets around

My perfect world
No wars at all
Lots of money
No maths for anyone
Wonderful drama
No literacy - *Boring*
Exciting dance yippee
No geography.

Shaunna Jolly (9)
New York Primary School

My Fabulous World

This is my perfect world
Vandalism no not at all
A cricket ground outside of course
Crooks not at all
Pets around
Flooding never around
Free electricity in every house
Never a cheeky little mouse!

My fabulous world
Perfect grass
No dentists at all
Banks everywhere
Surrounding all countries, is a wall
About fifty feet tall!

My fabulous world
No spellings at all
Literacy never
Loads of drama
Horrible maths extinguished
My fabulous world.

Tom Simmonds (8)
New York Primary School

The Fireworks

Fireworks raging in the sky
How do you fly so high?
How do you make a great display?
How do you blast a colourful ray?

I shoot up about a mile
I make so many children smile
Fireworks blasting coloured light
Could you make me a little more bright?

Josh Greener (10)
Redesdale Primary School

At The Football Match

The crowd cheers
The crowd claps
The crowd sings
The crowd chants.

The opposition boos
The opposition frowns
The opposition throws bottles
The opposition goes silent.

Lewis Keogh (11)
Redesdale Primary School

Fireworks

Fireworks in the sky
How can you sizzle and fly?
How many colours do you burst?
Why do you sizzle first?

Oh my friend
I will miss you when I end
I see faces smiling at me
I feel that I am free.

James Shek (10)
Redesdale Primary School

Children

Children are as good as gold,
They always do just what they're told.
You know that this is all a lie,
These things are evil, mean and sly.
They sneak up from behind,
You never know what's on their minds.
So heed my warning and beware,
The little devil might just be there!

Lauren Nicole Goodfellow (10)
Redesdale Primary School

Seven Bears

There were seven bears
Walking through the trees
The first was looking for honey
But got chased by the bees
The second went to sleep
The third was growling
And the fourth killed a sheep
The fifth tried to catch a fish
The sixth had a fight
The seventh looked for some meat
And quickly took a bite.

Alex Forman (11)
Redesdale Primary School

Seven Fish

There were seven little fish
Swimming in a tank
The first hit a rock
And then he sank
The second one was screaming
The third one was eating
And the fourth one's smile was beaming
The fifth wanted cover
The sixth wanted light
The seventh swam away
And now he might bite.

Amy Sutherland (10)
Redesdale Primary School

Seven Brothers Playing Football

There were seven brothers
Playing football
The first got tackled
And fell on the ball
The second ran all the time
The third wanted to be in goal
And the fourth shot at half-time
The fifth scored goals
The sixth went mad
The seventh ran away
And made everyone sad.

Dominic Ho (11)
Redesdale Primary School

Seven Seas

There were seven seas
Crashing against the land
The first turns pebbles
Into sand
The second sinks ships
The third is infested with sharks
And the fourth has a box saying chips
The fifth has a whirlpool
The sixth is full of lilies
The seventh is cold and icy
And makes everyone chilly.

Ben Durham (9)
Redesdale Primary School

Seven Soldiers

There were seven silly soldiers
Fighting on a battlefield
The first fell over
And lost his shield
The second went mad and got shot in the head
The third ran away
And the fourth lost his leg
The fifth wanted his dog
The sixth wanted his cat
The seventh saw a tank coming
And soon he was flat.

William Robson (10)
Redesdale Primary School

Seven Robots

There were seven robots
Driving different cars.
The first crashed out and hit the bars.
The second was tired and fell asleep.
The third was looking at a map
And the fourth hit his horn. *Beep! Beep!* Beep!
The fifth wanted petrol.
The sixth broke down.
The seventh flipped over and broke his crown.

Callum-Leslie Weites (10)
Redesdale Primary School

Homer Simpson

Does Homer Simpson get tired of eating food all the time?
Does he ever get bored of watching TV when it is fine?
Does he ever want to go and play in the garden with Bart?
Does he wish he could get out of his chair?

David Scott (9)
Redesdale Primary School

Seven Little Racing Cars

There were seven little racing cars
Driving in a race
The first broke down and lost the pace
The second started wobbling and lost a wheel
The third one spluttered
The fourth started gurgling
The fifth wanted petrol
The sixth wanted oil
The seventh skidded all around
And made everyone boil.

Darius Liu (9)
Redesdale Primary School

Bonfire Night

Bonfire Night please listen to me
Is it magic what I see?
Is it hard to catch alight?
I just love what's in my sight.

Bang! Whoosh! The noise is all the fun
I can't wait for all the people to come
Fireworks at the ready
Why am I so hyper? I have to stay steady.

Hannah Watson (10)
Redesdale Primary School

Monsters

Monsters flying through the air
Monsters with different coloured hair
Monsters throwing stones
Monsters dribbling footballs round cones
Monsters playing with sand
Monsters running overland.

Callum Heppell (10)
Redesdale Primary School

Amazing Puppies

Puppies, puppies are so crazy
Puppies are so cute
Some are sneaky
Some are naughty
That's why I love them so much.

Puppies are so mad
Puppies are so bad
Puppies are so sweet
Puppies are so brilliant
That's why I love them so much.

Emily-Rose Snowdon (10)
Redesdale Primary School

Fireworks

Exploding fireworks in the sky.
Why is it that you're so high?
Why is it that you're so bright?
What do you see on Bonfire Night?

I see scared faces looking ahead.
'Look at that one', a little boy said.
I only get used once a year
I wish it was more, I love it up here.

Sophie Dugdale (10)
Redesdale Primary School

Daisies

Do daisies get bored of standing in the grass all day?
Do they wish they can escape from the soil and play?
Do they get annoyed at people making daisy chains?
Do they ever wish they could live in the desert plains?

Melissa Stephenson (10)
Redesdale Primary School

Seven Soldiers

There were seven soldiers
Fighting on a battlefield
The first was hurt
And had to be healed
The second lost his gun
The third was running away
The fourth wanted his son
The fifth forgot to get out of bed
The sixth took a while to die
The seventh strapped himself to a rocket
And went up in the sky.

Jonathan Watson (10)
Redesdale Primary School

Seven Spiders

There were seven spiders spinning a web.
The first fell off and cracked his head.
The second spun the web.
The third ate a fly.
The fourth was a neb.
The fifth crawled to Mummy.
The sixth wanted to boogie more.
The seventh went to see a movie.

Errin Storey (9)
Redesdale Primary School

Pencils

Do pencils get sick of getting rubbed about?
Do they wish they could jump and shout?
Do they get tired of doing everyone's work?
Do you think when they get sharpened it really hurts?

Bethany Relph (11)
Redesdale Primary School

Seven Designers

There were seven designers
Stitching at a table.
The first pricked her finger
And shouted, 'Help me Mabel.'
The second went to help her
And lost her shoe
The third went to get her.
The fourth one was running
And she stood in dog poo.
The fifth tripped up and hurt her head.
The sixth cried for her dad.
The seventh shouted, 'Be quiet.'
And everyone was sad.

Becky Weightman-Brierley (9)
Redesdale Primary School

Seven Baby Dragons

There were seven baby dragons
Roaring in caves
The first ran away
Making awesome waves
The second breathing fire all through the dark
The third roared loudly
And the fourth ate a shark
The fifth wanted jewels
The sixth wanted gold
The seventh flew around
And made everybody cold.

Andy Chan (10)
Redesdale Primary School

Seven Swimmers

There were seven swimmers
Swimming in the pool
The first rolled over
And they called her a fool
The second went to eat her tea
The third dived underwater
And the fourth went out with Lee
And the fifth wanted her mummy
The sixth was mad
The seventh swam around everyone
And made everyone sad.

Natalie Wandless (10)
Redesdale Primary School

Seven Penguins

There were seven silly penguins
Standing on the ice
The first one went home
And had a bowl of rice
The second flapped
The third flew away
The fourth penguin had a nap
The fifth wanted fish
The sixth was sly
The seventh waddled and waddled
And made everyone cry.

Samantha Wright (9)
Redesdale Primary School

Seven Snakes

There were seven snakes
Sleeping underground.
The first fell off a rock
And bumped her crown.
The second ssssssss . . .
All through the night.
The third was loudly purring
And the fourth wanted to bite.
The fifth wanted to hibernate.
The sixth wanted to crawl.
The seventh rolled onto his dad
And turned really tall.

Jayson Hunt (9)
Redesdale Primary School

Seven Monkeys

There were seven monkeys
Talking in a tree
The first fell out
And bumped his knee
The second scratched his fleas
The third ate a banana
The fifth went nuts
The sixth went for a haircut
The seventh went on a walk
And found a hut.

Hannah Carr (10)
Redesdale Primary School

Seven Dinosaurs

There were seven dinosaurs
Swimming in a pool
The first thought swimming
Was very cool
The second splashed and made the others mad
The third swam under the water
The fourth didn't think it was so bad
The fifth wanted water wings
The sixth wanted fish
The seventh was hungry too
And beat him to the dish.

Michael O'Brien (9)
Redesdale Primary School

Seven Sausages

There were seven sausages
Sitting on the sun
The first leapt off
And landed in a bun.
The second burnt its skin.
The fourth came out of a tin.
The fifth started with the butchers.
The sixth was stolen by a dog.
The seventh was eaten by a man
Before a jog.

Jamie Hunt (9)
Redesdale Primary School

Seven Soldiers

There were seven soldiers
Standing on a bed
The first jumped up and down
And began to go all red
The second was snoring very, very loud
The third ran around making everyone cry
The fourth marched very proud
The fifth was tired
The sixth was hungry
The seventh was naughty
And got fired.

John Wright (9)
Redesdale Primary School

Seven Babies

There were seven babies
Sleeping in the cot
The first one screamed
And bumped his nose
The second cried for his mummy
The third one was singing
And the fourth called for his teddy bear
The fifth wanted his dummy
The sixth shook a rattle
The seventh woke them up
And they had a battle.

April Horner (10)
Redesdale Primary School

Seven Dancing Cats

There were seven dancing cats
Dancing on the floor
The first fell over
And danced some more
The second wanted to find a buddy
The third was hungry
The fourth wanted to study
The fifth was silly
The sixth had a bat
The seventh looked funny
He was wearing a hat.

Joshua McGregor (9)
Redesdale Primary School

Seven Soldiers

There were seven soldiers
Sitting round a fire
The first said nothing
And sat on a tyre
The second had a fight
The third was fast asleep
The fourth found a kite
The fifth ate egg and chips
The sixth shook his head
The seventh was using a pencil
And snapped the lead.

Ryan Orchard (10)
Redesdale Primary School

Seven Sausages

There were seven sausages
Dancing on the dance floor
The first one fell
On the door
The second stopped dancing
The third was grumpy
The fourth was happy
The fifth went crazy
The sixth waved his hands
The seventh stamped his feet
In time with the band.

Jordan Mishner (9)
Redesdale Primary School

Seven Brothers

There were seven brothers
Sitting on a log.
The first one ran
To a frog.
The second went into town
The third went swimming
And the fourth one almost drowned.
The fifth one wanted ice cream
The sixth wanted money.
The seventh went to the pictures
And saw a film called 'Sunny'.

Alex Lovell (9)
Redesdale Primary School

The Environment

What do you think is going on?
Well here's what I think
We're using too much rubbish
We're causing all our ice to sink.

Recycle paper, clothes and glass
Reduce the amount of trash
Reuse your clothes and shoes
Even your old satin stash.

Trains, aeroplanes and cars
This is it, we're in the wars
Use your bottles over again
Don't use your car, walk down your lane.

Don't forget your kerbit
Or your green bin
Join in, enjoy it
But don't forget to recycle your tin.

Matilda Noble (10)
St Agnes' School, Crawcrook

That Big Bully

Bully's the name
Just stay away from him
He can punch and tease
Yes, he's the big bully
Fighting is the game.

I got punched today
By the big bully
He scared me and grabbed me
Oh why is he the same
Like this every day?

Diane Curry (10)
St Agnes' School, Crawcrook

The Recycling Plan

Refill your recycling box with everything known to man
You can recycle almost anything, paper, plastic even a cola can.
Even though it sounds a bore, but you could save so much more.
Water, water everywhere, leave it running we don't care.
Now the time's come to make it stop and don't fill your bath to the top.
Thank the people who make the world a better place
So we've got to follow them, see that's the case.
Look at the trees, you can help turn them upside down.
Cars, trucks and definitely aeroplanes are all awful names
Because they're not doing their part or even doing their job to start.
TVs, lights and even more, turn them off when you go out the door.
Help save energy and other things and you can do anything
                                        except grow things.
Have you got clothes that are too small,
Don't worry we can recycle them all.
They will go to people who have none.
There you go, they're gone.
So please do all you can to help
If you do I've got 4 words to say
You rule at recycling!

Beth Rutherford (10)
St Agnes' School, Crawcrook

Make Haste Don't Waste

If we keep heading this way we're heading for trouble
Wasting tins and cans is costing us double
You're throwing away your body weight every seven weeks
So stop right now before global warming hits its highest peak.
We're killing rare animals one by one
We've got to stop now, once they're gone, they're gone.
I hope I've got my message out loud and clear,
So me and you and everyone can change our kids future.

Peter Dixon (11)
St Agnes' School, Crawcrook

Of Course You Can

Let's end all of our loss by not doing a damaging toss,
It's really easy if you try then you'll be flying like a butterfly,
Packaging is very bad when it all runs out, you'll be sad.
So listen up humans all around,
We all need to recycle before we get down,
Let's not waste water, plastic, paper and glass,
Don't go on long trips because it makes too much gas.
It's time to get down on our hands and knees
In case we don't have anymore wonderful seas,
The air around us is turning into smoke,
Let's help our world before we choke.
Reduce, reuse, recycle man,
Don't say no because of course you can!

Elisabeth Baker (10)
St Agnes' School, Crawcrook

Go Green

Reuse and reduce can all help the world, yes it really can,
But don't you forget the recycling van
Around it comes day after day
But be careful it only comes once in May.

Water is running out faster and faster
Turn off your tap while brushing your teeth
Then you'll be crowned the Water Master.

Stop cutting down trees
Just think of all those bees
We love animals so make sure they love you!

Sophie Howorth (10)
St Agnes' School, Crawcrook

The Angry Bully

They can blackmail
And they throw a rusty nail
They take drugs
And become evil thugs.

They threaten and kick
But it isn't funny when they come to nick
When they see me run
That's the bully's kind of fun.

They think it's funny when you are alone
Then they use the power of the mobile phone
When they steal from us
They throw it under the school bus.

Rian McLaughlin (10)
St Agnes' School, Crawcrook

The Bullies Crunch

Bullies, bullies they're just not funny,
When they take your money,
They can make you sad
Because bullies are bad.

When the bullies want fun,
Everyone starts to run,
My friend disappeared
And left me alone in tears.

The bullies punched
And made my body crunch,
The bullies are bad,
That's why I'm so sad.

Ryan Havery (9)
St Agnes' School, Crawcrook

My Life

A big bully fight
Just 'cause I'm scared of heights
What are you doing stealing my lunch?
Hey you, don't punch.

All I need is loving care
But children don't even dare
You go and spoil my game
Don't you feel any shame?

This is the thing
They think I'm disgusting
They lie and lie and lie
I wish they would die!

Katherine Milton (9)
St Agnes' School, Crawcrook

I Hate Bullies

I hate bullies,
They call me names,
They laugh at me,
And spoil my games.

I feel all sad,
I'm all alone,
No one likes me,
They sent me a text on my phone.

I tell on them,
They make me cry,
I need a friend,
They always lie.

Ruth Brickland (9)
St Agnes' School, Crawcrook

Cyber-Bullying Is Wrong

C is for crying which they force me to do
Y is for why do it to me?
B is for bully the master of cruel
E is for email from which there is no escape
R is for really hurtful to my feelings
B is for blubbering, which is what I often do
U is for unfair how it is on me
L is for how long it's been going on
L is for lonely sitting in that corner
Y is for yo-yo how it feels to be pushed
I is for Internet the bully's best place to be
N is for near me when they come close
G is for ganging up on me.

I is for invincible as he goes across the yard
S is for silly as bullying is this.

W is for worry what I often do
R is for reverse as I back away
O is for obsessed, this is what bullies do a lot
N is for never anyone else just me
G is for good but it's not for me.

Michaela Bousfield (9)
St Agnes' School, Crawcrook

Making Fun Of Me!

S is for swear as they shout at me
T is for take which they do from me
E is for my emotions that they bully
A is for attack which happens to me
L is for laughing, what they do when I cry.

Emily Gray (9)
St Agnes' School, Crawcrook

Bullies, Bullies Everywhere

I was kicked, I was punched
And they stole my packed lunch,
I stop and I stare
But they just shout and swear.

They forced me to take a drink and a drug
But they just laughed and called me a thug,
Everyone stares and stares at me
Because I'm being bullied by the big bad bully.

I tried to get away, seriously
But they just came and followed me,
Running down the corridors,
I think they're a bunch of wild boars.

It's school today, I'm still at home,
They try and call me on my phone.
They came over and tried to fight,
They know what's wrong, I know what's right.

Kathleen Phillips-Buck (9)
St Agnes' School, Crawcrook

The Magic Box
(Based on 'Magic Box' by Kit Wright)

I will put in the box . . .
A mirror with rubies and riddles on the frame,
A cute little kitten sitting on a coffee table.
I will put in the box . . .
The delicious smell of a million chocolate lands.
I will put in the box . . .
A beautiful crow singing in a small tree.
I will put in the box . . .
A delicious chocolate land.

Joseph Allan (8)
St Agnes' School, Crawcrook

The Bad Bullies

Bullying is bad not to mention it's sad
Other people think it's fun, it can get you done,
Everybody's scared but no one cared
They just bully and go but when the teacher asks
They just say 'no',
But they know inside that they lied.

Now who will they pick on?
Maybe that boy called John.
They think he's a wimp but he will take them on
And make them limp,
Taking them on is really wrong
But no one does, they just stay away,
Because they don't like what they say
And that's the sad story of the bullies.

Dominic Harrison (9)
St Agnes' School, Crawcrook

Help!

It was Monday morning
I said to my mum
I feel sick,
But I don't really
It's just a trick.

Mum said, 'Sorry you'll have to go.'
'Are you being bullied?'
I said no.
I start to cry,
I'm just worried.

Kasia Mackay (9)
St Agnes' School, Crawcrook

Feelings

You are the big bully, the one I fear
You kick me and punch me
Every time you come near
I feel so helpless, so scared
I want everyone to see.

Every time I see you, I am so worried
I am frightened, so hurt and upset
All I want is to keep my head buried
From the first time that we met
I've felt so invisible.

You pull me, you grab me and even steal
You think you're so strong and so very tough
I know all you want is to hurt how I feel
You've made me unhappy, so now that's enough
Please just stop or I will speak up.

Erin Stutt (9)
St Agnes' School, Crawcrook

Don't Bully

Do not bully,
Because it is bad,
It makes people sad,
You wouldn't like it.

So . . .
Do not bully because it is mean
And you wouldn't like it one bit,
But remember before you hurt
Someone think, would you like it?

Philip Butler (9)
St Agnes' School, Crawcrook

The Attack

They call me a freak,
But I do not speak,
They say they will hit me,
After they bit me.

I am afraid,
But I am not even scarred,
They beat me up, they are done,
They are gone.

They come back the next day,
I am not feeling well,
I try to run,
But they are not done.

They spit in my face,
That's a complete disgrace,
They are gone,
But not for long.

Alex Wildman (9)
St Agnes' School, Crawcrook

The Big Bad Bully

Bullies get you at school
They think they are so cool,
They take things you've got
Don't let them tie you in a knot.

Bullies are mean
But are hardly ever seen,
They don't care
Their friends just stand and stare.

It's a shame
They make it look like a game,
They try and try
To make you cry.

Erin Golightly (9)
St Agnes' School, Crawcrook

Bad Bullies

People who fight
Don't do right,
They're scary and mean
So tell a member of the adult team!

You feel invisible
And definitely miserable,
Tell someone your secret, please share
Or they'll keep pulling your hair.

You're all alone
And you want to phone,
Someone
Before there is more harm!

Tell someone now
And stop the row!

Becky Robinson (9)
St Agnes' School, Crawcrook

Bullying

When I went school one day,
I saw a kid being chased away,
I even saw him at lunch,
The horrible thug stole his packed lunch.

And at the end of the day,
He went far away,
Then I saw him on the street,
He gave the boy such a beat.

And even at night,
He started to chime,
'You're a loser',
Then he committed a crime!

Christy Bright (9)
St Agnes' School, Crawcrook

The Magic Box
(Based on 'Magic Box' by Kit Wright)

I will put in the box . . .
A dolphin swimming in the big blue sea
And a bird soaring in the air.

I will put in the box . . .
A snake hissing in the sand.
I will put in the box
Delicious sausages
And the smell of apple juice.

I will put in the box . . .
A sun burning in the fresh air.
I will put in the box . . .
A soft, fluffy kitten.

My box is fashioned from
Silk and little stars on the lid
With glitter in the corners.
Its hinges are covered with red roses.

I shall swim in my box through the great ocean
Then land on a little island.

Jennifer Reynolds (7)
St Agnes' School, Crawcrook

Injustice

B lackmail is fun, you can get cool stuff
L ike robbing a bank but much easier
A nd best of all they don't tell
C ause they're just too scared. Why?
K icking scares them to death
M y bat ought to frighten them
A nd when they run home
I say, 'Oi don't tell your mum
L ike yesterday or you're in for it!'

Keelan Kellegher (9)
St Agnes' School, Crawcrook

The Magic Box

(Based on 'Magic Box' by Kit Wright)

I will put in the box . . .
The roar of 20 tigers growling together,
A mermaid with long, soft, silky, golden hair,
White, pink and red roses
From a fragrant English garden.

I will put in the box . . .
The voice of a beautiful angel singing sweetly,
The first word of a baby,
Stars twinkling.

I will put in the box . . .
The love of all my family,
The smile of my dad,
The sight of a reddy-orangy
Brilliant blue sunset.

I will put in the box . . .
A whisk of the wild wink from the west,
The smell of melted chocolate,
Bunnies, chicks, panda bears,
Puppies, kittens and kangaroos, all babies.

I will put in the box . . .
All the friendship of my friends,
Dolphins performing tricks,
The splash of a wave hitting a rock.

My box is fashioned from
Rubies, diamonds, amethysts and pearls,
With golden and silver stars on the lid
And wishes in the corners.
Its hinges are the toes of tigers.

I shall fly in my box
With the breeze all around
The big blue sky,
Then land on a candyfloss cloud
And float with angels forever.

Sarah Baker (7)
St Agnes' School, Crawcrook

The Magic Box

(Based on 'Magic Box' by Kit Wright)

I will put in the box . . .
A chocolate fountain that has caramel in it,
A slither of a snake strolling along the muddy ground,
A cloud growling with rain and rage.

I will put in the box . . .
Flicking of pages when you turn them over,
Cracking of sweets when you crunch them,
Blossom that bees carry beautifully.

I will put in the box . . .
A game of chess that will never end,
A bird's feather as soft as a baby's blanket,
A silky white horse that will take me to a faraway land.

I will put in the box . . .
A crispy wanton that is made from jelly beans,
A spicy pepper that has lava in it,
A crunchy strawberry that has bubblegum in it.

My box is fashioned from
Beautiful butterflies all different colours
And wrapping paper,
With diamonds on the lid.
Then I will fly to the desert.

Lucy Roddam (8)
St Agnes' School, Crawcrook

Stop The Bully

S is for sadness, that's how I feel
T is for terrible, I'll get the cops
O is for odd, you people are strange
P is for pulling my hair and my tops.

I is for invisible, yeah that's how I feel
T is for try to be friends, not fight.

Daniel Allan (9)
St Agnes' School, Crawcrook

The Magic Box
(Based on 'Magic Box' by Kit Wright)

I will put in the box . . .
The deepest blue river you could ever imagine,
The running of a cheetah lost in a storm,
A sparkling igloo in a huge pile of snow.

I will put in the box . . .
The first tweet of a baby bird,
A bark of a tiny puppy,
The sound of the loudest elephant in the world.

I will put in the box . . .
A pancake downstairs waiting for me to eat,
The smell of petrol in a quiet garage,
The smell of sizzling sausages in a pan.

I will put in the box . . .
The tiny little fairy hand that came from Neverland,
The head of a ghost that had not been seen for years,
My mam's red lips.

I will put in the box . . .
A little bit of salty water from the sea,
The taste of toast,
The taste of fish and chips.

My box is fashioned from silver icicles and steel,
With diamonds on the lid and TVs on the corners.
Its hinges are the jaws of a dragon.
I shall fly to Pluto in my box
Then climb the highest mountain.

Bethany McLaughlin (7)
St Agnes' School, Crawcrook

The Magic Box

(Based on 'Magic Box' by Kit Wright)

I will put in the box . . .
A big shiny amazing fast pet.
I will put in the box . . .
A very noisy school class.
I will put in the box . . .
Bacon rashers sizzling in the pan.
I will put in the box . . .
The taste of a sweet juicy orange.
I will put in the box . . .
The white fluffy snowflakes.
My box is fashioned from ice shells and diamonds
With stars on the lid and memories in the corners.
Its hinges are ice cubes.
I shall turn invisible and scare my teacher
Then land on the moon and have tea with the aliens.

Harvey Jack (7)
St Agnes' School, Crawcrook

Here Comes The Bully

S is for spitting on me
T is for tease me every day
O is for often hitting me
P is for please stop.

B is for bullying people all the time
U is for upsetting which I feel every day
L is for lying on the floor
L is for laughing at me
Y is for why do you hurt me?
I is for ill which they make me
N is for nagging me
G is for ganging up on me.

Joe Urwin (10)
St Agnes' School, Crawcrook

My Magic Box

(Based on 'Magic Box' by Kit Wright)

I will put in the box . . .
A swimming splashing mermaid.
I will put in the box . . .
A teensy baby crying in the air.
I will put in the box . . .
Some bacon sizzling in a big blue pan.
I will put in the box . . .
The end of a sticky gluestick.
I will put in the box . . .
A beautiful pink flower.
My box is fashioned from beautiful big red hearts
With huge shiny moons on the sides.
Its hinges are ribbons and jokes in the corners.
I shall dance up to the top of a mountain
Then I'll end up in a magical cave
With fairies and goblins.

Chantelle Christensen (7)
St Agnes' School, Crawcrook

The Frightened Little Girl

They are totally bad
And I'm totally sad
I try to greet them like a friend
But they only beat me and push me away.

The next time I saw them I said
'Hey you, I want to stay today
I don't want to run away'
But they don't listen.

They punch me and slap me
I'm sad, totally sad
I run away
Never wanted to stay.

Marlie Corble-Robson (9)
St Agnes' School, Crawcrook

The Magic Box

(Based on 'Magic Box' by Kit Wright)

I will put in the box . . .
A dog playing football.
A tiger leaping in the long grass.

I will put in the box . . .
A cat chasing a bird, running after spiders.

I will put in the box . . .
A horse and a tiger.

I will put in the box . . .
Gold and money.

I will put in the box . . .
A zebra, a pirate and a zebra on a pirate's ship.

My box is fashioned from . . .
Gold and silver with gold and emeralds on.
Its hinges are dinosaur bones.
I shall ride up the biggest ramp on my bike
then land on the top.

Matthe Hamill (7)
St Agnes' School, Crawcrook

Fear

Bullies, why do they do it?
They are not funny
Filming my fear
Kicking me, punching me
Whenever I'm near.

You lurk in the shadows
I run away
Just wait one day
I will get my own way.

Katie Stuart-Brown (9)
St Agnes' School, Crawcrook

The Cat

Sleepily, the cat nestled into the cushion,
All happy, next to the radiator,
She dozed off, contentedly,
Deep in the cushion.

Much later in the night, she stirred,
A cold draught brushed her face,
She woke up,
She stretched and went outside.

Softly and silently, she slid through the partly open door,
She sneaked into the moonlit garden,
There, she stalked through the shadowy flower beds,
She prowled past the pond,
Stretched proudly,
A queen of the velvet night.

Suddenly, she heard a dog across the deserted garden,
She arched her back,
Hissed into the darkness,
She spat her anger,
Then slunk off into the shadows, unconcerned.

Sophie Thorpe (9)
St Agnes' School, Crawcrook

Bully At School

There's a bully at school
He steals everyone's stuff
Then he plays with them and
His friends video it on their phones.

At night he comes to my house
And throws eggs at my windows.
If I tell an adult will he try to bully me more?
It has to be worth the risk.

Tom Ellis (9)
St Agnes' School, Crawcrook

The Cat

The sleepy cat
Curled up in a ball
Next to a radiator
Cushion and all

Much later in the night
A breeze brushed her face
She blinked and twitched
With great annoyance

She sneaked silently
As she proudly crept out
And sidled softly and strutted
When she stalked about

Aware of a dog
Somewhere in the fog
Slowly miaowed
Miaow!
Miaow! Miaow!

Lucy King (9)
St Agnes' School, Crawcrook

He's Coming

Oh no the bully, he's coming
The sound of fear is drumming
He always, always pulls my hair
And all of these people just sit and stare.

He spits in my eye
I would rather die
He's going to get me
I am so lonely.

He cut me with a knife
I nearly lost my life
But now he's in jail
That is my sad tale.

Jackson Maddison (9)
St Agnes' School, Crawcrook

Young Writers - Little Laureates Poems From Tyne & Wear

The Magic Box

(Based on 'Magic Box' by Kit Wright)

I will put in the box . . .
Sausages running down the street.
A hot day.

I will put in the box . . .
A land of white chocolate.
A T-rex roaring in my box.

I will put in the box . . .
Anything with chocolate in.

I will put in the box . . .
16 new footballs.

I will put in the box . . .
A new expensive car.

My box is fashioned from . . .
Gobstoppers, gold and silver
With sweets on the lid.
Games in the corner.

The hinges are sweets with extra sugar on.
I shall fly to Mars and get a Mars bar
Then I shall skateboard on sparkling ice.

William Watson (7)
St Agnes' School, Crawcrook

The Bully

They kick
And make you feel sick.

They punch
And eat your packed lunch.

They take drugs
And become horrible thugs.

They call you names
And spoil your playground games.

Jack Thompson (9)
St Agnes' School, Crawcrook

The Magic Box

(Based on 'Magic Box' by Kit Wright)

I will put in the box . . .
A dolphin leaping out of the sparkling water.
I will put in the box . . .
The first squeak of a baby guinea pig.
I will put in the box . . .
The smell of a bacon sandwich with mushrooms.
I will put in the box . . .
The softest fur of a newborn puppy.
I will put in the box . . .
Chocolate cakes and fairy cakes just cooked.
My box is fashioned from
Dazzling stars and rubies on the lid
With sparkling memories and wishes.
Its hinges are mouths of fairies.
I shall dream in my box
Then make a wish.

Lucy May Wood (7)
St Agnes' School, Crawcrook

Stop Bullying

S is for sadness
T is for teasing
O is for often punching me
P is for pushing and pulling.

B is for bullying
U is for upsetting
L is for laughing at me
L is for lying when I've been punched
Y is for yelling in my ear
I   is for irritating me
N is for nagging me
G is for ganging up on me.

Kayleigh Grant (9)
St Agnes' School, Crawcrook

The Magic Box

(Based on 'Magic Box' by Kit Wright)

I will put in my box . . .
An active puppy running and jumping,
Barking and enjoying his walk.
I will put in my box . . .
A hot crackling, burning fire.
I will put in my box . . .
A rushing, powerful, running waterfall.
I will put in my box . . .
A nice hot bag of chips
With a dollop of ketchup on it.
I will put in my box . . .
The touch of swishing grass.
My box is fashioned from sparkling royal jewels
And the finest diamonds
And pure gold with silver on the lid.
I shall surf in my box on the sea of the ocean
Then jump ashore onto a beach.

Alice Brown (7)
St Agnes' School, Crawcrook

The Bully

S top the bully
T hey are all around
O ften in the playground
P lease make it stop.

B ig boys attack me
U psetting me at school
L et's play the right rules
L ook, please make it stop
Y ou could be my friend
I could be your friend too
N o, he says
G o away, he says.

Harry Carver (9)
St Agnes' School, Crawcrook

The Magic Box

(Based on 'Magic Box' by Kit Wright)

I will put in the box . . .
A beautiful, unusual, unbelievable, fantastic and amazing canter
on the best pony in the world
and a newborn foal whinnying for the very first time.

I will put in the box . . .
The laugh of a baby for the first time ever.
The clop of a pony trotting.

I will put in the box . . .
The best perfume in the world,
body spray and petals.

I will put in the box . . .
A furry pony, a silky dolphin and my mum's lips.

I will put in the box . . .
A sweet lollipop chocolate, salad, love and ice cream,
melted ice cream with chocolate sauce.

My magic box is fashioned from pony fur,
cold ice and the finest cream with chocolate on the lid
and butterflies in the corner.
Its hinges are metal covered with cotton wool.
I shall canter in my box then surf the Atlantic Ocean.

Katie Lawson (7)
St Agnes' School, Crawcrook

Terrible Bully

I'm being bullied
By a terrible kid
He pulls my hair
It doesn't feel fair
He spits in my eye
I would rather die.

Bethany Caffrey (10)
St Agnes' School, Crawcrook

The Magic Box

(Based on 'Magic Box' by Kit Wright)

I will put in the box . . .
A baby sleeping in a cot.
A colourful butterfly flying on a nice summer's day.
A nice beautiful flower growing from a seed.

I will put in the box . . .
In the morning when the birds sing.
A water fountain that is spraying water at me.
A blue wave that is splashing on a nice sunny summer day
                                                    at the beach.

I will put in the box . . .
The smell of toast drifting everywhere.
The smell of soap powder that is in the magic washing machine.
The smell of fresh orange that has just been made.

I will put in the box . . .
A cute little soft bunny who is just asleep.
A soft fluffy candyfloss cloud.

I will put in the box . . .
A lovely taste of melting chocolate in your mouth.
The taste of fish and chips, it's delicious.
The taste of ice cream melting, freezing cold in your mouth.

My box is fashioned from stars in the moonlight
With icicles twinkling by the cold ice.
Its hinges are the toes of a cute, soft little bunny.
I shall fly in my magic box over the moon far over the stars
Then land on a beach the colour of the sun.

Corinna Grant (7)
St Agnes' School, Crawcrook

The Magic Box

(Based on 'Magic Box' by Kit Wright)

I will put in the box . . .
Fire from the nose of a Chinese dragon.
The tip of a T-rex's tooth.
Chestnut shell shining on the tree.

I will put in the box . . .
The sounds of a piano playing beautifully.
A volcano erupting.
A massive splash in a puddle that drenches me.

My box is fashioned with beautiful birds on the lid
and clouds in the corners.
Its hinges are shells.
I shall surf in my box
then land on a trampoline.

Michelle Reid (8)
St Agnes' School, Crawcrook

Help Me

S is for a silly big idiot
T is for my tears
O is for ow!
P is for please stop I'm in pain.

B is for the bully who thinks he is cool
U is for upset and scared
L is for look at my wound
L is for leave me alone
Y is for you sick bully
I is for feeling ill
N is for nobody plays with me
G is for he grabs me and swears.

Adam Charlton (10)
St Agnes' School, Crawcrook

The Magic Box

(Based on 'Magic Box' by Kit Wright)

I will put in the box . . .
A massive cauldron of blackberry spiders,
A colourful rainbow in the clearest sky,
Birds singing.

I will put in the box . . .
Juicy blackberries,
Swishing waves on a rocky beach,
The soft fur on a baby cat.

I will put in the box . . .
A roller coaster spinning around,
A crazy gorilla running around,
The smell of my mum's perfume
When she tucks me in to bed.

I will put in the box . . .
Delicious ripe strawberries,
A splashing waterfall,
A tiny brown puppy with spiky ears.

My box is fashioned from
Jewels, diamonds and sequins
With diamonds in the corners
Balloons on the lid.
Its hinges are the horn of a unicorn
A toe of a dinosaur.

I shall go to the moon
Then I shall go to fairy land.

Faye Parker (7)
St Agnes' School, Crawcrook

The Magic Box

(Based on 'Magic Box' by Kit Wright)

I will put in the box . . .
A baby badger digging with its paws
And a wild rabbit jumping across Jamaica
And a water bear trying to get some fish from the silky lake.

I will put in the box . . .
A water fountain splashing through the stones
Nuts with caramel and a chocolate fountain
With fruit peaches, lemon and lime.

I will put in the box . . .
A panda curling up in my arms
And a kangaroo chasing me.

The box is fashioned from flowers and gorgeous hearts
With ice that can never melt.
Its hinges are a jaw joint of a dolphin.

I shall fly in my box and swing on the lovely
Rose trees, lilies, roses and pansies!
Then I shall get a star and it shall fly up to the moon
To its star family!

Sarah Rutherford (7)
St Agnes' School, Crawcrook

Help Save Our World

R ubbish is recreating our world
E verywhere piles of rubbish are getting bigger and bigger
C limate change, think we've got to help our world
Y ou can help as well
C reate a better world for us
L ittle things can help us
I   f we work together recycling will be on everyone's mind
N eed reactions quickly, keep
G oing this will help our world.

Izzy Sherborne (10)
St Agnes' School, Crawcrook

The Cat

Softly and sleepily
The cat nestled into the cushion beside the warm radiator
She curled
Up into a small ball
And fell into a deep sleep and dozed contentedly.

Much later in the night she stirred
In the cold draught
She awoke in annoyance
And yawned lazily and stretched in the darkness.

Softly and silently she slid through the partly opened door
And sneaked into the moonlit garden
Quickly and cautiously she prowled
Through the flower beds and past the pond
She leaped onto the garden wall
She strutted proudly as queen of velvet night
Suddenly aware of a dog across the deserted gardens
The cat frowned
She hissed into the darkness
Then she spat and slunk off into the night.

Georgie Mackay (8)
St Agnes' School, Crawcrook

Compost Bin

C ompost is black so is my bin.
O bviously you should have a full compost bin, if you don't
                                    your flowers will be dead.
M um don't do that, put it in the compost bin, you'll like that.
P op in my head 'Please do that, put it in the recycle box'.
O ff in the bin don't do that, too much packaging, recycle that.
S ick of all the world, make it a better place, put everything in
                                    the right place.
T o make a good place, do what you have to do, so put
                              everything in their place.

Fabrizio Stifanelli (10)
St Agnes' School, Crawcrook

The Magic Box

(Based on 'Magic Box' by Kit Wright)

I will put in the box . . .
The last mist on a misty night,
The last bundle of a bundled ball of string,
The last charm of an ancient uncle.

I will put in the box . . .
Newcastle winning a football match,
My favourite food like delicious chocolate,
The first laugh of a baby.

I will put in the box . . .
The first woof of a dog,
The speed of a motorbike on the highway
And a snowman.

I will put in the box . . .
Some lava,
Some ice,
Some snow.

I will put in the box . . .
Some rainbow fairy dust,
A beautiful rainbow
And some pearls fresh from the sea.

aMy box is fashioned from pearls and oysters,
Rubies, stars and the sun,
With wishes in the corners and secrets on the lid.
Its hinges are crescent moons.

I shall surf on lava in my box,
Then I shall end up in a magic tunnel in the side
                              of the volcano.

Adam Davidson (7)
St Agnes' School, Crawcrook

The Magic Box

(Based on 'Magic Box' by Kit Wright)

I will put in the box . . .
A Chinese fan with a key in it covered in sapphires.
A butterfly's eyelash, small and silky.

I will put in the box . . .
A rainbow sun with unusual colours like rush red and gurty green.
A roar of a mouse and a squeak of a lion.

I will put in the box . . .
A cloud roaring with laughter as it rains on all the people.
A very special wave filled with all the blues.
A rainbow swirl full of colours and a butterfly's wing.

I will put in the box . . .
A thousand seeds especially from a giant land.
Every sugar plum fairy from the violet sky.
Red, gold and silver.

I will put in the box . . .
Petals from flowers with turquoise sea in.

My box is fashioned from
Unicorn horns, rubies, sunsets, lions' hearts and seashells,
With the swish of a scarlet sari on a summer night.
Its hinges are crafted from peacocks' feathers.

I shall fly in my box to a magical place far, far away
To a land of queens and princesses.
Then land on a tropical island and sail away in a
                                        beautiful sunset.

Bethan Hobson (7)
St Agnes' School, Crawcrook

The Cat

A cat was soft, warm and snugly,
While she was asleep,
Next to the radiator she rolled into a ball
And stretched very tall.

Later at night she felt a dark deep draught
And suddenly awoke,
Her anger was rising,
She took a long breath
Then shook herself awake.

She heard a noise of a bark and got up,
She slid through a gap in the door,
She chased it away,
Into a bush,
She came out
And needed a brush.

Jenny Hetherington (8)
St Agnes' School, Crawcrook

The Cat

Softly the cat lay down in her bed
And curled herself into a cosy ball
She slipped into the softening warmth
Dozed her brain until she slept.

Later she came awake
She twitched her tail
Blinked in annoyance

She sneaked through the door
And into the night
She wanted someone
Someone to fight

She heard a noise and twitched her tail
She spat her anger at the distant noise
Into the bush she crept alone.

David Guy (8)
St Agnes' School, Crawcrook

The Cat

As the cat slept
Next to the radiator
She purred softly into the moonlight
Then she dozed off into a deep sleep

Into the night a cold draught came
She constantly shivered
She woke up suddenly
And stretched out to her full length

While the draught went past
She slid through the open door
And walked through the moonlit garden
In silence like black ink

She heard a dog bark
As quickly as possible
She jumped into a bush
Then ran back to her home.

Megan Dawson (8)
St Agnes' School, Crawcrook

The Cat

The sleepy cat curled in a ball
Next to the radiator
Purring and dozing

She was awoken
By a cold draught
Her whiskers twitched softly and silently

Suddenly a dog came running towards her
Startled awake
She ran for her life
She turned and spat
At the snarling dog.

Myles Croxford (9)
St Agnes' School, Crawcrook

The Cat

As the cold wind blows
The cat is warmed by its fur
At the fireplace she lies
Near a gentle flame.

Suddenly the cat wakes and
Blames her stomach
She tries to find some food
She sees a mouse
It leads her into next-door's garden.

She searches for hours on end
Her stomach leads her into next-door's garden
Suddenly she hears a dog
She hisses a beware signal
The dog casually turns and leaves.

Zhandos Kearney (8)
St Agnes' School, Crawcrook

The Cat

A cat slept on a cushion beside the radiator
Curled into a cosy ball
Later, in the night,
She shivered
In a freezing frost of cold
Softly and silently
She started to stand
She slid into the garden
And jumped on a high wall
She was amazed
A dog stood in her flower bed
She spat her anger and then retired.

Sean Henry (8)
St Agnes' School, Crawcrook

The Cat

Sleepily, the cat curled
Against the radiator
Then she happily dozed off.

Later a cold breeze
Brushed her hair
Touching her face.

Suddenly, she woke up
Her whiskers twitched
And she stretched herself
Awake in the darkness.

There was a noise
It came from a bush
Out came a dog
She hissed at it
Then turned away.

Aimee Stamp (8)
St Agnes' School, Crawcrook

The Cat

The cat was curling on a cushion.
She fell asleep beside the radiator
She was very content.
She awoke and drank slowly,
Suddenly, she heard a noise.
She got up and licked her paws and purred.
She went outside, walked softly in the garden.
She jumped in fright
It was a dog,
She hissed at him
Then turned back home.

Kirsty Wright (8)
St Agnes' School, Crawcrook

The Cat

A cat sleepily curling on a cushion beside the radiator,
Curling into a cosy ball.
Purring softly as she snuggled into the soft warmth,
Dozing off contentedly.

Later in the night she stirred in a cold draught,
Twitching her whiskers.
Blinking in annoyance and yawning lazily,
Stretching herself awake in the darkness.

Softly and silently she sidled through the partly open door,
Sneaking into the moonlit garden.
Stalking through the shadowy flower beds
She strutted proudly, a queen in a velvet night.

Aware of a dog somewhere across the deserted gardens
Arching her back,
Spitting her anger at the distant enemy,
She slunk into shadows unconcerned.

Megan Rubbi (8)
St Agnes' School, Crawcrook

The Cat

The cat curled up and went to sleep,
She nestled in a cushion,
She was so deep in a sleep,
She didn't even leap.

Much later in the night,
She woke up and had a fright,
There was a cold and awful draught,
Her whiskers twitched with annoyance.

Softly and silently she straightened her back,
And sidled through the partly opened door,
Entering the night like liquid jet
She resembled a velveteen queen.

Catherine Baker (8)
St Agnes' School, Crawcrook

Help The Environment

When you've finished the paper what do you do?
You put it in the recycling bin and say yahoo!
100 million tons of waste is dumped every year
So let's help the environment and show we care.

30 million pounds of aluminium is paid every day
We don't want that, so don't throw it away.
Use paper both sides whenever you can
Don't use one because you are breaking my plan.

Reduce, reuse, recycle, can you do that?
He can do it, that man with the hat.
Use a compost bin for grass and old food
If you do that you'll be crowned my dude.

Plastic, plastic it's all a waste
When you wrap something only use what you need.
Companies and shops give us what we require
But of plastic and packaging, we are starting to tire.

Michael Harrison (10)
St Agnes' School, Crawcrook

Save The Earth!

Come on, come on let's save the Earth,
If we all start recycling you can help preserve,
The thing our children are growing up in,
Start composting food scraps, don't put 'em in the bin.

The water cycle is looking grey,
So turn off your tap straight away,
Turn off your dishwasher, use some elbow grease,
And lots of our troubles will cease.

Rubbish dumps are getting full,
If it spills out of our land, it will really look dull,
Ride on your bike to school today,
Then without any worries we can start to play.

Caitlin Gray (10)
St Agnes' School, Crawcrook

Dream!

Not remaking but recycling doesn't affect the Earth.
If every day we recycled it would be a more healthy world.
I wish everybody could use the three R's, reduce, reuse and recycle.
I hope my dream comes true, it's very important to me and you.
Please recycle, reuse and reduce, it's for our own good.
To see natural beauty being destroyed just when we could recycle.
It's such a disgrace, don't let it happen or global warming
will harm us!

Brendan Richardson (10)
St Agnes' School, Crawcrook

Recycle

Recycling is good
Each year the UK produces more than 100 million tons of scrap
Dispose your fruit, keep a healthy nation
Use the other side of paper
Can you remember what the 3R stands for? -Reduce, reuse
and recycle

Environment needs clean air, let's help get it.

Rachel Findley (10)
St Agnes' School, Crawcrook

Let's Recycle

R educe, reuse, recycle is all you have to do.
E verybody in the world can recycle too.
U se your brain and recycle now.
S o start recycling then take a bow.
E veryone who is reading this please take heed, do as I say
and then you've done a good deed.

Jessica Dawson (10)
St Agnes' School, Crawcrook

The Recycling Poem

Everybody stop and take a look around
100k up to the sky.
Take a look along the ground
Is the air fresh and clean?
Is there wildlife everywhere?
Are you proud of what you see?
Do you really think you care?

Think carefully before you throw away
Your paper, bottles and jars
Could it be used in another way
To save this planet of ours.

Have you seen how much waste is in the sea
It is caused by you and me
There is bottles, wrappers and plastic
If you stop this you'll be Miss Fantastic
Is this hard to do
It's fair because it's made by you.

Coleen Mary Huntley (10)
St Agnes' School, Crawcrook

Please Help Our World

R ecycling rubbish around the world.
E arth is filling up with fumes.
C reate a better world for us!
Y ou can help too!
C limate change around the world, help our Earth fast
L ittle things can help!
I n and out the cities you go, get the water running now.
N o don't waste water, it's getting too late the Earth is
                        becoming an awful state.
G ain your energy to help our world quick!

Bethany Oliver (10)
St Agnes' School, Crawcrook

You're Polluting The Planet!

The world is a very special place
And it was very safe
Until we went and made a mess
It was the very, very best
The environment is rotting away
So be careful what you say
The packaging on special presents
Will save you lots of pennies
Unlike lots of peasants
You have more than enough
Of polluting the planet like a scruff
The water all around us
Is sinking each day
So turn your tap off I hear your mum say
Everyone do your bit
To save the world from going down a dip
So be careful what you do!

Charlotte Mann (10)
St Agnes' School, Crawcrook

Recycle! Recycle! Recycle!

The Earth is feeling sad
Because our recycling is very bad.
We throw everything away
Why can't they stay?
If you keep things like bottles and tins
There will be a lot of grins.
Your life is great
But the Earth's in a bad state.
Give the Earth care
If you want to waste, don't you dare!
If we do everything that's good
We'll do it, I'm sure we could!

Ricky Macis (10)
St Agnes' School, Crawcrook

The Recycling Poem

All around the world to be,
All around you'll see,
With rubbish burning all around,
In your streets and in your town,
End the days,
With a happy gaze,
For you and your friends have done
A great job,
Not out there polluting the world with
A big mob,
In this poem I hope you have learned
And I hope your pollution has overturned,
Keep the world from being a mess,
It's not really a big test,
So don't be lazy and sit around,
Help the world and your town.

Elle Croxford (10)
St Agnes' School, Crawcrook

Recycle The Earth

What do you think is going on?
Recycling bottles, cans, glass and paper too
Come on, there's a lot to do.
People everywhere are throwing their paper and cans
And are destroying the Earth when you can recycle.

Stop cutting down the trees for this paper
Monkeys are dying and being injured
So please stop!
Don't throw away your leftovers
Get a compost bin and use it for your roses.

Niamph Gilmore (10)
St Agnes' School, Crawcrook

Recycling World!

Recycle,
Think about our future,
Act now,
Nearly everything can be recycled.

Think about it,
Recycle those bananas, paper and skins of a pear,
Everyone has to do their bit,
I really care.

The world is getting warmer,
So let's start recycling
Or one day will be like melting icicles.

Help me now
Or we'll get stuck,
In a world without any luck.

Erin Mann (10)
St Agnes' School, Crawcrook

Environment

E verything you can recycle, recycle
N ever waste anything
V andalism will ruin our Earth
I n your house most things are reusable
R ecycling will save more things
O bviously people need to recycle more
N o don't put it in the bin, recycle it and then you
                              will be crowned the king
M ake the world better and put everything in its place
E arth is a ball of a rubbish tip
N earby trees are getting cut down so recycle
T ry to keep the Earth as it should be, then when your
                work is done, sit down and have a cup of tea.

Tori Houckham (10)
St Agnes' School, Crawcrook

Autumn Breezes

As I stand in the autumn air,
My clothes are fluttering everywhere.
As the golden leaves fall off the tree,
Gold, red and brown is all I can see.

The trees are rocking,
As the branches are knocking.
The breeze blows a Mexican wave through his hair,
As the breeze sends a message to the mayor.

The breeze is getting stronger,
I can't hold any longer.
The conkers are dropping,
The trees are rocking and the leaves are floating.

Autumn breezes are as strong as a feather tickle,
Children play in leaves as they laugh and giggle.
Now it's Hallowe'en, the night is getting spooky,
As the breeze blows a chocolate chip cookie.

If you listen carefully you will hear the weeping willows cry,
The singing breeze or the 'crunch, crunch' band of leaves

but I have a sigh.

Stella Robinson (10)
St Catherine's RC Primary School, Sandyford

Jim Jarvis' Feelings In A Poem

I have now the opportunity,
To make my escape real,
Now my friend has left me,
I don't know how I feel.

Deep down inside of me,
It was the right thing to do,
Think about it long and hard,
What would you do if I were you?

I feel so confused,
To why my friend left me so,
I would do anything to leave,
Even if it meant being poor.

Now I'm approaching the gate,
All in a muffle,
I decided I would be strong,
And run not shuffle.

I am halfway through,
The black solid gate,
To get caught,
That's what I would really hate.

So I dart through the gap,
And sprint the rest,
Being out in the wild,
It really is the best.

I can now hear the footsteps,
Of people passing by,
Now all I need,
Is a great big sigh.

My lungs are filled with air,
I am finally free,
From all the nasty work,
Escape was meant to be.

Alicia Youens (10)
St Catherine's RC Primary School, Sandyford

Winter

Trekking through the cold white snow,
I wonder why I'm going slow,
Breathing in the freezing air,
The wind running through my hair.

Sledging fast down the hill,
There's no time when I'm standing still,
Flying snowballs all around,
Carol-singers are not the only sound.

Looking through the icicles,
Winter's full of miracles,
Wear your hat, your scarf and gloves,
For the snow looks like peaceful doves.

Snowboarding is so much fun,
Because the winter's just begun,
Winter is my favourite season,
Now you know I have a reason.

Rebecca Wood (10)
St Catherine's RC Primary School, Sandyford

My Monkey Ike

I once had a little monkey
Who followed me to school
My teacher said I was crackers
I said, 'No his name is Ike you fool'.

At my house he ruined the garden
As well as eating all the food in the fridge
Ike is a friend, a very good friend
But he can be a bit annoying too.

In literacy today we had to write a poem
I wrote about Ike and said
'Never buy a monkey as a pet
They are a lot of trouble you know'.

Esme Cawley (8)
St Catherine's RC Primary School, Sandyford

Dragon Panic

Today in our school
A very strange thing happened,
A dragon came through our door and said
'Is this really St Catherine's?'

Everyone ran away
But I was glued to my seat,
And then I said to the dragon
'I am glad that we can meet'.

He went into the yard
And it was very bare,
Then the dragon breathed fire
And it burnt off all my hair!

I got very angry
And he saw smoke coming from my ears
It scared him away and I don't think
He will come back any other day.

Jasmine Little (9)
St Catherine's RC Primary School, Sandyford

Always Listen To Children

My lion was hungry
So I gave him Cheerios.
I told my teacher all about him
She didn't believe me and kept me in

So the very next day
I brought him to school.
The playground emptied quickly
I wonder why that was so

It gobbled her up
Once and for all
I bet she tasted like Brussels sprouts.
The lion gave out a loud smelly burp.

So teachers watch out
Teachers beware
If children tell you about their strange pets
Listen carefully or else.

Lily Rose Oliver (8)
St Catherine's RC Primary School, Sandyford

The Chimney Sweep

Ragged trousers, dusty face
I'm brushing soot in every place
Up the chimneys day by day
I love this job in every way
Lighting candles
I love the smell
I love this job, can't you tell?

I always brush up and down
I dream that I have the crown
I dream at night and through the day
I'm the best at my job
In every way.

I take a candle with me
To light up the dark
It isn't really big
Just a little spark
Now this is the end of my story
Oh, I could tell much more
But I have quit my job as sweeper
And now I'm working for the law!

Josie-Leigh Donkin (9)
St John Bosco Primary School, Sunderland

The Lonely Chimney Sweep

There was a chimney sweep called Ben
Who always wanted a den
So to fulfil his wish
And carrying a knife, fork and dish
He hid in the chimney there and then.

Dana Deary (9)
St John Bosco Primary School, Sunderland

The Old-Fashioned Chimney Sweep

Little children with dirty faces
Clothes that are ragged and old
Pushing their bodies in very tight spaces
When it's freezing cold.

Only a flame of a candle to see
There's no electricity to guide me
Cleaning chimneys isn't for me
Oh how I long to be free.

We get shouted at all day
If we don't work fast
We only get a break in the month of May
I need more money for food to make me last.

Scabs on dirty feet
Scars on my face
On the street there's no warm heat
I wish I had a little warm place.

Caitlin Henderson (9)
St John Bosco Primary School, Sunderland

The Life Of Tim The Chimney Sweep

There once was a chimney sweep called Tim.
He really was very slim.
He ate a little mouse.
That lived in his house.
Oh that chimney sweep was very dim.

James Watt (9)
St John Bosco Primary School, Sunderland

The Dead Sweep

The chimney sweep, the chimney sweep,
Have you ever heard of the chimney sweep?
With ragged clothes and bony legs
A blacked out face, for food he begs.

The chimney sweep, the chimney sweep,
Have you ever heard of the chimney sweep?
With scabs on his feet
From the intense heat
Have you heard of the chimney sweep?

The chimney sweep, the chimney sweep,
Have you ever heard of the chimney sweep?
The straggly lad
Who's never been bad
Have you heard of the chimney sweep?

The chimney sweep, the chimney sweep,
Have you ever heard of the chimney sweep?
He cleaned his last chimney last week
Fell down his ladder and now we weep
Have you heard of the chimney sweep?

Ben Clark (10)
St John Bosco Primary School, Sunderland

Poor Bill

There was a chimney sweep called Bill
The scabs on his feet would kill
He spent day and night
Up a great height
It really was a great thrill.

Ryan Donnellan (9)
St John Bosco Primary School, Sunderland

Chimney Sweeping's My Game!

Chimney sweeping's my game,
Billy Black is my name.
Climbing up chimneys is so sweet,
You have to be light on your feet.
Chimney sweeping's my game.

Brushing out soot, what a shame,
This job is really lame.
My chest is in so much pain,
Chimney sweeping's my game.

My clothes are ragged and torn,
I start work at five in the morn.
Ten chimneys a day is my aim,
Chimney sweeping's my game.

I work Monday to Friday,
I don't get a big pay.
Everyone knows my name,
Chimney sweeping's my game.

Here I am about to die,
I was just a boy who was very shy.
I will never have any fame,
Chimney sweeping was my only game.

Tom Walker (9)
St John Bosco Primary School, Sunderland

Will's Short Chimney Sweep Life

There was a chimney sweep called Will
His master's name was Phil
He never slept
Because he swept
Poor Will died of a winter's chill.

Sarah O'Connor (9)
St John Bosco Primary School, Sunderland

Chimney Sweeping In The Rain

I work in the chimneys
I get covered in soot.
My master tells me
To work and shut up.

I work in the day
And work in the night.
I'm tired and restless
With my shining light.

A lot of the times
I am stuck in the rain.
Inside then outside
With an awful pain.

I look down a chimney
It is pitch-black.
I better hurry
Or I'll get the sack.

My master says
I am such a pain.
If something goes wrong
I get all the blame.

Lauren Garner (9)
St John Bosco Primary School, Sunderland

Wolves

W olves are not house pets.
O rder in the pack is highly used.
L ook in a forest and you might find it
V ery noisy at the sight of the moon
E very morning hunting begins
S tocks of food are always there
                standing before them.

Jack Bell (9)
St John Vianney Catholic Primary School, West Denton

My Friend

My friend is sweet,
So am I.
She plays with me all the time,
We have never broken up at all.

My friend almost never forgets,
Only sometimes, but I do.
She is really funny,
I don't know about me.

My friend is happy,
So am I.
She helps me when I am down
So do I.

My friend and I are very close.

Anya Nelson (9)
St John Vianney Catholic Primary School, West Denton

My Dad Loves To . . .

My dad loves to bake,
He makes the most delicious cakes.
My dad loves to read,
About all different breeds.
My dad loves to play,
Especially when we're at the bay.

My dad loves to love,
The crystal-white doves.

My dad loves to whizz about,
He even likes Brussels sprouts.

My dad loves everything except himself.

Robyn McNulty (9)
St John Vianney Catholic Primary School, West Denton

Night-Time

N ight is dark
I   am playing in the park
G iggle in the night, giggle all day
H iggle and squirm, time to play
T ime to go to bed because it's night-time.

T wisting and twirling all night long.
I f I were you I would sing a little song.
M y features are I never go to bed.
E lephants jumping in my head.

Jasmine Kidd (9)
St John Vianney Catholic Primary School, West Denton

Flowers

F lowers are bright, flowers that are red and white.
L ovely flowers blowing in the wind.
O n the grass in the sunlight.
W eather does not matter because flowers are always there.
E verywhere in the world, flowers are always there.
R epeating, growing again and again
S hining brightly in the sun all day long.

Olivia Killen (9)
St John Vianney Catholic Primary School, West Denton

Lions

L ions are fantastically fierce.
I n the jungle they live and they are on top
O n top they are a king
N ever weak, they streak to their prey
S o when they reach their prey, they see and want to kill.

Jack Harrington (10)
St John Vianney Catholic Primary School, West Denton

Fireworks

F ireworks are bright and colourful.
I maginative and colourful fireworks.
R iding themselves high into the sky.
E asy to see the flying colourful dots.
W ow! People shout when they're in sight.
O ur fireworks shining in the night.
R ound about the clouds, fireworks shine bright.
K aboom! The fireworks are shining in the night.
S uper fireworks shining bright.

Adam Barnett (9)
St John Vianney Catholic Primary School, West Denton

Dancing

D ancing is really fun
A dance is easy to make up
N ice to dance for other people
C lever to do tricks in a dance
I 'm a brilliant dancer
N ice to dance across the stage
G olden medal around my neck.

Emily Patterson (10)
St John Vianney Catholic Primary School, West Denton

Dragon

D ragons are vicious things.
R ed-hot fuming fire they blow.
A scary beast dragons are.
G iant and scary monsters they are.
O f all the monsters, I think dragons are the worst.
N othing is as scary as a dragon.

Andrew Coffell (10)
St John Vianney Catholic Primary School, West Denton

The Graceful Snow

The snow lay covering on the ground
It gracefully fell without a sound
The silent chime of a distant clock
The snow lay covering up my block

I begged my mam to come outside
I asked and asked until I cried
A small red scarf and a pretty hat
The snowman stood beside the cat.

Then suddenly all became most clear
The Christmas trees and the reindeer.
Red and green are the holly leaves.
I realise now it is time to receive.

Amy Hawkins (10)
St John Vianney Catholic Primary School, West Denton

Who Am I?

I am brown, I swing in the trees, I make a funny noise,
Who could I be?

I eat one fruit, it is yellow, it begins with a 'b',
Who could I be?

I go *ooh-aah* all night long,
I am non-stoppable,
Who could I be?

Giggling and squirming with my friends,
I carry a baby on my back,
Who could I be?

A: I am a monkey.

Emily Davis (9)
St John Vianney Catholic Primary School, West Denton

My Life

My life is great in my swimming pool,
swimming all day long.
My life is want, want, want,
what I never get.
My life is day by day going on and on
in the beautiful sunshine.
I cry all day long.
My life has gone so far along,
I miss those great days.
My life is *sob, sob, sob,*
when my family's gone.
My life is *tock-tock,*
when my kids play under the big sun.
My life is small when my family's grown,
and sob, my life goes away.

Emily Armstrong (9)
St John Vianney Catholic Primary School, West Denton

Fireworks

Fireworks crash and smash
Incredible colours blasting in the dark sky
Random crashing sparklers
Enormous bonfire burning away
Wonderful colours shooting across the sky
Original colours bashing about
Rushing colours into the sky
Kaboom! Watch the rockets soar into the air.
Sparklers whizz round and round.

Luke Walton (9)
St John Vianney Catholic Primary School, West Denton

I'm A . . .

I'm a brass lock.   I'm a brass key.
I'm a yellow lock.   I'm a yellow key.
I'm a small lock.   I'm a small key.
I'm a cool lock.   I'm a cool key.
I'm a big lock.   I'm a big key.
I'm a funny lock.   I'm a funny key.
I'm a girl lock.   I'm a girl key.
I'm a happy lock.   I'm a happy key.
I'm a sad lock.   I'm a sad key.
I'm a monk lock.   I'm a monkey!

Aimee Duncan (9)
St John Vianney Catholic Primary School, West Denton

Life On A Star

If I lived on a star
I would run around and look for Mars
Dancing around trying to get back my breath
I could jump from one world to another
I would brighten up the planet
From all around
People would stare at me from afar . . .
If I lived on a star.

Sarah Balmain (9)
St John Vianney Catholic Primary School, West Denton

What Colour Are Roses?

R oses can be different colours but you normally say they are red.
O range roses are pretty as well.
S talks of roses are bright green.
E xcellent roses growing in my garden.
S pringtime roses are beautiful.

Jessica Burgess (9)
St John Vianney Catholic Primary School, West Denton

Love

If love were an animal it would be a beautiful swan.
If love were a colour it would be gold and white.
If love were food it would be tasty and healthy.
If love were a person it would be pure and fair.
If love were an ornament it would be romantic and sweet.
If love were a sound it would be the graceful sound of a violin.
Love is as bright as the sun.

Joanna Hodgson (10)
St John Vianney Catholic Primary School, West Denton

My Friend The Unicorn

U nderneath his pointy horn his shiny teeth gleam,
N icely he gallops through the grass,
I nstead of being nasty he really is nice,
C an you gallop like the brave and beautiful unicorn?
O n the back of the unicorn his pink and white fur sways in the breeze,
R unning sweetly his tail swishes in the wind,
N obody has the horn of my friend the unicorn.

Bree Dalton (9)
St John Vianney Catholic Primary School, West Denton

Dancing

D azzling is my groovy pink and black dance costume,
A nd moving and moving until my feet hurt.
N ice spotlights shining on me.
C an I get any more clapping from the wonderful audience?
I ncredible hair, I just can't get better.
N ever, ever, am I going to stop.
G olden trophy in my hands.

Emily Walton (9)
St John Vianney Catholic Primary School, West Denton

Life

Life is short so I'm going to get on with this,
Life is great.
It's magic, without life
I would be a whole new person.

Life, life, life,
Life is lovely, it is the most enjoyable experience,
It would be horrible without
Life.

Life, life, life,
Life is fun, life is fabulous, make the most of your life,
Life is the most beautiful thing of all.

Jessica Hall (9)
St John Vianney Catholic Primary School, West Denton

Life

Life can be easy
Life can be hard
Sometimes things work
And sometimes they don't.

I wonder what will happen in 500 years
Will we be walking on walls
And drinking from cars?
Will we be green
Or will we be cream?
I wonder
I wonder
I wonder.

Kate McHugh 10)
St Mary's RC Primary School, Forest Hall

My Weird Two Weeks

With two weeks till summer, I was sitting at my desk
Bored as usual I was looking out the window not doing my best
Then I noticed something weird
It was a dragon burning flowers and it had a beard
The next few days it did the same
Then it went away after a few hours jumping around like it was
                                                    playing a game
At the weekend I went to the park next to the school
I saw a phoenix flying, its eye was like a big jewel
On Monday I woke up and remembered one week
                                        till summer
At school I saw something that looked and sounded like a drummer
From Tuesday to Friday I saw some weird creatures
That ranged from basilisks to things that looked like leaches
That Monday after I woke up, was it all a dream?
I looked out the window, *huh!*

Zachary Hui (10)
St Mary's RC Primary School, Forest Hall

My Grandma

My grandma is the best.
She is cool, fun and brilliant.
She never complains, even when it's raining.
She helps me with my problems
And knows just what to do
She puts others before herself
Yes, my grandma is the best
And that's
True!

Lauren Napier (10)
St Mary's RC Primary School, Forest Hall

Seasons

In the early morn of spring,
Absolutely everything,
Is given life to start anew,
Oh, and what a view.
Fawns leaping all around,
Plants sprout from the ground.
Baby birds learn how to fly,
Fox cubs let out a cry.

In midday of summer,
An elderly guitar strummer,
Sings and plays upon the sand,
While kids hold ice creams, in their hands.
Many try to relax and swim,
While people, usually quite slim,
Try to get a perfect tan,
So steamy they need 10 fans.

In the afternoon of fall,
Leaves, so very small,
Fall from withering trees,
Caused by the autumn breeze.
People cooking bacon nicely,
They have to fry it so precisely,
For the Queen is coming to tea,
That's why there's a fuss you see!

At midnight of wintertime,
No, he isn't committing a crime,
Santa Claus comes down to send . . .
That's how the seasons end!

Eleanor Osada (10)
St Mary's RC Primary School, Sunderland

Groove To The Music

Dance to the beat,
Follow your feet.
Groove to the floor,
Dance some more.
Do a twirl,
Your hair will curl.
Have a good time,
Listen to the chime.
As it comes to the end of the day,
You have to pay.
But it was all worth it,
You were a massive hit.

Francesca Shanks (10)
St Mary's RC Primary School, Sunderland

Snow

Snow, snow
How I do like the snow,
It lies like a white, soft blanket,
Over all that I know,
Snow, snow, snow.

Snow, snow
It's soft and cold,
And everyone thinks it's fun,
But I can't wait for the sun,
Sun, sun, sun.

Daniel Forrest (11)
St Mary's RC Primary School, Sunderland

A Poem About Greek Gods

There were three great Greek Gods,
Named Ares, Hades and Zeus,
Who wanted to solve a mystery
And went out to find the clues.

They went to ask Poseidon for help,
But Poseidon's dead body was down,
The three great Greek God's reaction,
Was a really big frown.

So they went to Athena,
Because she was so wise,
But her dead body lay on the floor,
And was being eaten by flies.

They took turns to guard,
And heard a big surprise,
Even though the two Gods were dead,
They could still hear their cries.

Then they went back to Athena,
Who had come back to life,
She said save Dionysus,
Who might be killed with a knife.

So they went to Dionysus,
Who was paralysed with shock,
They saw creatures in the shadows,
Who were took down with a hard knock.

But the creatures got up,
And put up a big fight,
But they were beaten,
In the morning light.

Callum Bradfield (10)
St Mary's RC Primary School, Sunderland

Countries

Ciao from Italy and little Sicily,
The boat shaped country,
Pizza and pasta,
Venice and Roma, ciao!

Bonjour from France,
We're French at a glance,
Mattise and Monte,
Il feit du soleil, au revoir!

Ola from Spain,
Madrid is Spain's main,
Castanets and maracas,
Sangria and tapaz, adios!

Howdy from the States,
Where the cowboys are ya mates,
Disney and Hollywood,
Pecan pie's a scrummy pud, laters!

Konnichiwa from Japan,
The festival of the fan,
Tokyo and Mount Fugi,
Noodles and sushi, sayonara!

Hello from England,
My town is Sunderland,
Bulldog and hedgehog,
Conkers and leapfrog, bye!

Meriel Smithson (10)
St Mary's RC Primary School, Sunderland

Cars

The engine churning,
The fan turning, the wheels spinning fast.
The shiny paint on the new car.
With the indicators flashing in the dark,
All the children stood and stared at the car whilst playing
in the park.

The wheels racing round the track,
The only thing that it would lack would be . . . nothing,
It would be perfect all round.
There would be no sound from the engine, that would in
other cars be loud.
From this car there would be no sound.

Daniel Simpson (10)
St Mary's RC Primary School, Sunderland

A Rabbit's Tale

Behind the cage I lie and wait,
Until the time you open my gate,
I'm small, I'm fast, my feet are quick,
I'm very good at performing a trick,
Flash back and forth, to and fro,
Scoot under bushes watch me go,
I have a name tag around my neck,
My name is Thumper, would you like to check?

Sam Hope (10)
St Mary's RC Primary School, Sunderland

Winter Playground

I can hear the children's laughter in the air
Blowing against me
And the crispy leaves being kicked about on the ground
I felt as cold as a frosted snowman
And as fragile as a leaf blowing in the icy wind.

I could see the children playing in the snow
Making a snowman like a dog chewing a nice juicy bone
I can feel the cold snow blowing in my face
I am standing alone.

The playground was full of laughing children
And playing nice winter games
The sound of cheering
And everywhere I looked, everywhere was nice
It was like a wave hit me
Because everyone seemed to melt like ice.

Holly Hazell (9)
Sea View Primary School

The Day Of Misery

I can see children screaming
With pleasure and delight
Children as happy as a dog with a bone
Every child longing to be home.

An icy blast of wind touched my face
Leaf as smooth as paper
Children race
I feel as a snowman in the snow
Feel like a fragile leaf.
Why will nobody play with me?

Dylan Ford (9)
Sea View Primary School

The Playground

The playground was as cold as icicles.
Children shouted and screamed.
Sound of trees and voices
Swishing everywhere you go.

The playground was as slippery as ice.
Friends playing all around
Feeling cold yet safe.
All about playing and having fun.
The playground was buzzing with fun!

Scott Davison (9)
Sea View Primary School

Loneliness

Lonely is the colour of blue
Lonely tastes like fish that's sour
Lonely smells like dark rotten leaves
Lonely looks like a dark cupboard
Lonely sounds like nothing, an emptiness
Lonely feels sad, lost, miserable.

Chloe Kingsland (9)
Sea View Primary School

Love

Love is red,
The taste of sweet strawberries,
Love smells like new flowers,
And looks like a picnic on the grass,
Love sounds like a love song,
It feels like the touch of a delicate rose,
Love is sweet!

Megan Galloway (9)
Sea View Primary School

I'm Too Impatient

Grey will pay for my impatient problem
My impatient problem does taste like toxic wastes
I think it smells like rusty old bells
It looks like millions of ducks
I think it sounds like a big herd of clowns
The emotion does show that I go with the flow
My impatient problem is not my blame
Such a shame
My impatient problem is going away.

Alisha Kirtley (9)
Sea View Primary School

Playground Fun

The playground was like an adventure for me
I can see children playing happily.
As happy as a dog with a bone
Saying hello.

The playground was like a whole lot of fun.
Hearing screams of laughter.
Voices are carried in the wind.
Feeling like a roller coaster.

Chloe Stephenson (9)
Sea View Primary School

The Past Is Sad

Sad is dark blue
Sad tastes like sour grapes
It smells like smoke
Looks like dirty puddles on the ground
Sounds like a baby crying in the rain longing to be warm and safe
Feeling like walking in the wind and the rain.

Danielle James (9)
Sea View Primary School

Winter is Here

Children playing happily
Having snowball fights
Little frozen icicles on the fence.
The leaves on the ground
It is such a shame
They were my pride and joy
But I'm not the blame.

The touch of snow on my knees
It gives me a blasting chill.
The frozen football touches my shoe
And rolls off in the snow.
The sound of fading leaves
In the distance, it is very calm.

I feel as cold as a lonely snowball
Lost in a dream.
Winter is here.

Marley Luther (9)
Sea View Primary School

Playground Puzzle

The playground is like a prison to me.
It feels as cold as a frosted snowman.
I feel alone like a leaf blowing in the breeze.
I see children as happy as can be.

The play is like a forest to me.
Friends were playing and I'm alone.
Leaves are blowing in the wind.
I hear screams of laughter.

I can touch the icy blast of wind touching my face
And the leaves scattering on the ground.
A hand reaches and I am warm.

Shannon Robinson (9)
Sea View Primary School

Playground Joy

One cold frosty day
I was left alone
No one to see, no one to play
No one sitting next to me.

I fell like a frosty winter leaf
An icy blast of wind
Touches my face
My mind begins to race.

A friend swished by like an autumn leaf
Now I am not alone
I hear screams of laughter
Realise it's me.

Stevie Brooks (9)
Sea View Primary School

Happy

Happy is blue.
Happy smells like
Chocolate toffee,
Delicious.
Happy tastes like pickled
Onion crisps
Happy looks like caramel
Oozing.
Happy sounds like
Screaming at the fair.
Happy feels like
Chocolate in my mouth.
Happy is what I want to be.

Brandon Riley (9)
Sea View Primary School

Harder Than

Harder than a table
Harder than gold
Harder than a coconut tree
Harder than a big grey rock
Harder than an axe cutting wood
Harder than a saw
That's how hard my sister punches me!

Joshua Smith (8)
Valley Road Community Primary School

Louder Than!

Louder than! A television on full volume
Louder than! An aeroplane crashing
Louder than! A bully bashing
Louder than! A tree falling
Louder than! A bad man calling
That's how loud I can burp!

Clayton Gough (8)
Valley Road Community Primary School

Quieter Than

Quieter than a mouse tiptoeing
Quieter than a cheetah sneaking
Quieter than eggs smashing
Quieter than the breeze blowing
Quieter than a teddy bear
That's how quiet my baby sleeps.

Ryan Ganley (9)
Valley Road Community Primary School

Softer Than

Softer than a baby's bum
Softer than a woolly teddy
Softer than some cotton wool
Softer than a feather
Softer than a fish in water
Softer than a bit of fluff
That's how soft my mum's skin is.

Tialeoni Thompson (8)
Valley Road Community Primary School

Louder Than

Louder than a motorbike
Louder than a drill in action
Louder than a big bass drum
Louder than an eagle screaming
Louder than a lion roars
That's how loud my sister screams!

Jimmy Hall (8)
Valley Road Community Primary School

My Verb Poem

It was so quiet that I heard a cat running
Across the garden chasing a mouse.
It was so quiet that I heard a leaf uncurl
Like a green tongue when it was falling from the tree.
It was so quiet that I heard a butterfly's wings
As it was flying about my garden.

Sara Robson (8)
Valley Road Community Primary School

Faster Than

Faster than a cheetah
Faster than a shark
Faster than a motorbike or a shooting bullet
Faster than a quadbike
Faster than a train
Faster than an aeroplane and a bulldozer in action
Faster than a boulder falling from a cliff
Faster than a hurricane blowing
That's how fast my dad can run.

Nathan Reay (9)
Valley Road Community Primary School

Softer Than

Softer than a fluffy sock
Softer than a baby's vest
Softer than a fluffy rabbit
Softer than a glass of milk
Softer than cat's fur
Softer than a teddy bear
Softer than a feather pillow
Softer than a dog's ear
That's how soft my mummy's cuddle is!

Elle Young (8)
Valley Road Community Primary School

Young Writers Information

We hope you have enjoyed reading this book - and that you will continue to enjoy it in the coming years.

If you like reading and writing poetry drop us a line, or give us a call, and we'll send you a free information pack.

Alternatively if you would like to order further copies of this book or any of our other titles, then please give us a call or log onto our website at www.youngwriters.co.uk

Young Writers Information
Remus House
Coltsfoot Drive
Peterborough
PE2 9JX

(01733) 890066